Ontology of the Accident

Ontology of the Accident

An Essay on Destructive Plasticity

CATHERINE MALABOU

Translated by Carolyn Shread

polity

First published in French as *Ontologie de l'accident* © Éditions Léo Scheer, 2009

Reprinted 2013, 2014 (three times), 2015, 2016 (twice), 2017 (twice)

This English edition © Polity Press, 2012

Polity Press
65 Bridge Street
Cambridge CB2 1UR, UK

Polity Press
350 Main Street
Malden, MA 02148, USA

ISBN-13: 978-0-7456-5260-3
ISBN-13: 978-0-7456-5261-0 (pb)

A catalogue record for this book is available from the British Library.

Typeset in 11 on 15 pt Adobe Garamond
by Toppan Best-set Premedia Limited
Printed and bound in the United States by LSC Communications

The publisher has used its best endeavors to ensure that the URLs for external websites referred to in this book are correct and active at the time of going to press. However, the publisher has no responsibility for the websites and can make no guarantee that a site will remain live or that the content is or will remain appropriate.

Every effort has been made to trace all copyright holders, but if any have been inadvertently overlooked the publisher will be pleased to include any necessary credits in any subsequent reprint or edition.

For further information on Polity, visit our website: www.politybooks.com

"We must accept the introduction of the *aléa* as a category in the production of events. There once more we feel the absence of a theory enabling us to think the relations between chance and thought."

Michel Foucault, "The Order of Discourse"

Translators' prefaces, more often than not, are designed to parry accidents of translation. Yet, rather than excusing myself or warning readers about discrete glitches or fault lines running through this English version of Catherine Malabou's text, in this brief preface I would like instead to think of translation itself as accident. What if translation were to accept the accident as its condition, its condition of possibility, its possibility? And what if the change of course that may occur to any text in translation were understood as a change beyond difference? Putting aside the equation of similarities and differences, the plastic equilibrium between a giving and a receiving of form, the accident that lies beyond difference is, I have come to understand in translating Malabou's *Ontology of the Accident,* the ontology of translation.

Translation is often parsed in terms of a positive plasticity that gives and receives form, that modifies, meta-morphosizes, transforms or mutates, along with the host of attendant gains and losses. By contrast, an accidental translational ontology assumes also destructive plasticity, an explosive plasticity that evokes fear and is used to justify security measures and normative strictures that seek to delimit the field of translation, and against which translation studies butts its head time and again. Yet far from protecting against accident, it may be that the conventional protocols that aspire above all to neutrality in translation are those that are responsible for its most serious accidents, by splitting the translator's reason from her affects. That translation is prone to accidents, bound as it is to a degree of destruction, accounts for its poor status and the widespread deprecation of this form of writing. Generally, we put up with translation from necessity; what if instead we delve into the pleasures of departure . . .

> *Ô Rumeurs et Visions! Départs dans l'affection et le bruit neufs !* (Rimbaud)

. . . for whatever precautions are taken, the change that translation practices is always liable to uncover the uncanny, the change that unsettles identity, inspiring horrified fascination, ridicule or repulsion.

As it happens, in Malabou's *Ontology of the Accident,* we experience this same discomfort – even in the French. In her steely confrontation of the disconcerting power of being to change, Malabou calls readers to envisage their own possible accident, the transformation that leaves them dumb and disoriented, departed. Drawing on literature as an ally willing to face the decomposition and regeneration that ontology describes – the ontology in which being is becoming – Malabou explores areas where we hesitate to tread except in the company of trusted guides, or from the shelter of the text. As I followed her again in this third translation, my art moved beyond the difference that is but an extension of identity to meet the possibility of its accident.

The explosive accident is terrifying, terrible. And yet, as Malabou points out, the possibility of such accidents is with us at every moment of our lives. However much our course is mapped, there is always the chance of the freak event or minor detour that reroutes us. Much as we wish for a translation that would never trip up, a translation lying seamlessly next to its source, to take on a translation is to take on the accident.

Because translation is so closely enmeshed in the ontology of the accident, eventually, thanks to Malabou's unpacking of this ontology, we may come to acknowledge that translating has something to offer beyond a means to an end. An embracing of translation as a practice that goes beyond pragmatics could alter the voice of translators as mediators of change. Translation might then assume its ontology as a valid mode of being in the world – a mode of being that is becoming.

Carolyn Shread

In the usual order of things, lives run their course like rivers. The changes and metamorphoses of a life due to vagaries and difficulties, or simply the natural unfolding of circumstance, appear as the marks and wrinkles of a continuous, almost logical, process of fulfillment that leads ultimately to death. In time, one eventually becomes who one is; one becomes only who one is. Bodily and psychic transformations do nothing but reinforce the permanence of identity, caricaturing or fixing it, but never contradicting it. They never disrupt identity.

This gradual existential and biological incline, which can only ever transform the subject into itself, does not, however, obviate the powers of plasticity of this same identity that houses itself beneath an apparently smooth surface like a reserve of dynamite hidden under the peachy skin of being for death. As a result of serious trauma, or sometimes for no reason at all, the path splits and a new, unprecedented persona comes to live with the former person, and eventually takes up all the room. An unrecognizable persona whose present comes from no past, whose future harbors nothing to come, an absolute existential improvisation. A form born of the accident, born by accident, a kind of accident. A funny breed. A monster whose apparition cannot be explained as any genetic anomaly. A new being comes into the world for a second time, out of a deep cut that opens in a biography.

Some metamorphoses disrupt the snowball that one forms with oneself over lived time, that big round ball: full, replete, complete. These strange figures rise out of the wound, or out of nothing, an unhitching from what came before. These figures do not arise from an unresolved infantile conflict, nor from the pressure of the repressed, nor from the sudden return of a phantom. There are some transformations that are attacks on the individual. I have written at length about the phenomena of destructive plasticity, of split identities, sudden interruptions, the deserts of Alzheimer's patients, the emotional indifference of some who have suffered brain injury, those traumatized by war, victims of natural or political catastrophes. We must all of us recognize that we might, one day, become someone else, an absolute other, someone who will never be reconciled with themselves again, someone who will be this form of us without redemption or atonement, without last wishes, this damned form, outside of time. These modes of being without genealogy have nothing to do with the wholly other found in the mystical ethics of the twentieth century. The Wholly Other I'm talking about remains always and forever a stranger to the Other.

In the usual order of things, lives run their course like rivers. Sometimes they jump their bed, without geological cause, without any subterranean pathway to explain the spate or flood. The suddenly deviant, deviating form of these lives is explosive plasticity.

In science, medicine, art, and education, the connotations of the term "plasticity" are always positive. Plasticity refers to an equilibrium between the receiving and giving of form. It is understood as a sort of natural sculpting that forms our identity, an identity modeled by experience and that makes us subjects of a history, a singular, recognizable, identifiable history, with all its events, gaps, and future. It would not occur to anyone to associate the expression "cerebral plasticity" with the negative work of destruction (the type of destruction wreaked by so many cerebral lesions and different traumas). In neurology, deformations of neuronal connections, breaches in cerebral contacts, are not considered instances of plasticity. Plasticity is only evoked when there is a change in the volume or form of neuronal connections that impacts the construction of personality.

No one thinks spontaneously about a plastic art of destruction. Yet destruction too is formative. A smashed-up face is still a face, a stump a limb, a traumatized psyche remains a psyche. Destruction has its own sculpting tools.

It is generally agreed that plastic construction cannot take place without a certain negativity. To return to the example of neurobiology, the reinforcement of synaptic connections, an increase in their size or volume, occurs when connections are solicited regularly, producing what scientists term "long-term potentialization." This is the case, for instance, in learning to play and practicing the piano. But of course this phenomenon has its opposite: when they are rarely or never used these same connections diminish. This "long-term depression" explains why it is more difficult to learn to play an instrument in later years than in childhood. Construction is counterbalanced by a form of destruction. This much we know and accept. The fact that all creation can only occur at the price of a destructive counterpart is a fundamental law of life. It does not contradict life; it makes life possible. As biologist Jean Claude Ameisen notes, the sculpting of the self assumes cellular annihilation or apoptosis, the phenomena of programmed cellular suicide: in order for fingers to form, a separation between the fingers must also form. It is apoptosis that produces the interstitial void that enables fingers to detach themselves from one another.

Organic matter is like the sculptor's clay or marble: it produces its refuse and scraps. But these organic evacuations are absolutely necessary for the realization of living form, which ultimately appears, in all its density, at the cost of their disappearance. Again, this type of destruction in no way contradicts positive plasticity: it is its condition. It serves the neatness and power of realized form. In its own way it composes the life force. In psychoanalysis, as in neurology, a plastic brain or plastic psyche is one that finds the right balance between the capacity for change and the aptitude for remaining the same, between what is to come and memory, between the giving and receiving of form.

It's an entirely different matter when it comes to the possibility of explosion, the annihilation of equilibrium, the destruction of this capacity, this form, this force, this general identity. Terrorism versus apoptosis. As I said, in these instances no one calls it plasticity any more. Even if the destructive and disorganizing explosive power is present virtually in each of us, ready to manifest itself, to take body or self-actualize at any moment, it has never received a name in any field whatsoever.

Never has the power of ontological and existential explosive plasticity for subjectivity and identity been granted an identity. Approached but avoided, glimpsed often enough in fantasy literature but never connected to reality, neglected by psychoanalysis, ignored by philosophy, nameless in neurology, the phenomenon of pathological plasticity, a plasticity that does not repair, a plasticity without recompense or scar, one that cuts the thread of life in two or more segments that no longer meet, nevertheless has its own phenomenology that demands articulation.

Phenomenology indeed. Something *shows itself* when there is damage, a cut, something to which normal, creative plasticity gives neither access nor body: the deserting of subjectivity, the distancing of the individual who becomes a stranger to herself, who no longer recognizes anyone, who no longer recognizes herself, who no longer remembers her self. These types of beings impose a new form on their old form, without mediation or transition or glue or accountability, today versus yesterday, in a state of emergency, without foundation, bareback, sockless. The change may equally well emerge from apparently anodyne events, which ultimately prove to be veritable traumas inflecting the course of a life, producing the metamorphosis of someone about whom one says: I would never have guessed they would "end up like that." A vital hitch, a threatening detour that opens up another pathway, one that is unexpected, unpredictable, dark.

6

1

Let's start with the fact that rarely in the Western imaginary is metamorphosis presented as a real and total deviation of being. Perhaps never once has it been seen in this way. However bizarre the metamorphoses may be—the most striking are found in Ovid—the forms they create, the result of the transmutations of the poor wretches who are its victims, remain, so to speak, very much in the order of things. After all, it is only the external form of the being that changes, never its nature. Within change, being remains itself. The substantialist assumption is thus the travel companion of Western metamorphosis. Form transforms; substance remains.

In Greek mythology Metis, the goddess of cunning intelligence, "changed herself into all kinds of forms": "a lion, a bull, a fly, a fish, a bird, a flame or flowing water."[1] But still, her polymorphism is not infinite. It comprises a vast but finite palette of identities. When Metis runs dry, she must quite simply restart the cycle of her transformations, with no possibility of further innovation.

Back to the start for the ruse. The returns of Metis cease with the drying up of the register of animal forms and this is why the other gods are able to triumph over her. If her metamorphic power were not limited, she would be invincible.

But this limit is hardly the failing of Metis alone. All the metamorphic gods systematically meet the same fate. All forms of transvestitism are included within a "range of possibilities" that can be catalogued and for which it is always possible to propose a typological schema, a panoply or sample.[2] Thus, for example:

> When the god is taken by surprise, in order to escape he assumes the most baffling of forms, those which are most at variance with each other and most terrible; in quick succession he becomes flowing water, a burning flame, the wind, a tree, a bird, a tiger or a snake. But the series of transformations cannot continue indefinitely. They constitute a cycle of shapes which, once exhausted, returns to its point of departure. If the monster's enemy has been able not to lose his grip, at the end of the cycle the polymorphic god must resume his normal appearance and his original shape and retain them thereafter. So Chiron warns Peleus that whether Thetis turns herself into fire, water or a savage beast, the hero must not lose his hold until he sees her resume her first form.[3]

8

Likewise, Eidothee warns Menelaus against the ruses of Proteus:

> Hold him fast no matter what he may try in his burning desire to free himself; he will assume every kind of form, will transform himself into whatever crawls upon the earth, into water and into divine fire; but you must hold on to him without flinching and grasp him even more tightly; and when in the end he will reach the point of agreeing to speak he will reassume the features you saw him to have when he was sleeping.[4]

Metamorphoses circulate in a cycle that links them, surrounds them, arrests them. Again, this is so because metamorphoses never carry off the true nature of being. If this nature, this identity were able to change deeply, substantively, then there would be no necessary return to prior forms, the circle would be broken, since what came before would suddenly be lacking in the ontological tangent it pursued. Transformation would no longer be a trick, a strategy or a mask always ready to be lifted to reveal the authentic features of the face. Transformation would betray an existential underground, which, beyond the round of metamorphoses, would enable the subject to become unrecognizable. Unrecognizable less because of a change in appearance than on account of a change in nature, a molting of the inner sculpture. Only

9

death can end this plastic potential, a plasticity whose tricks are exhausted by nothing and that never reaches "the end of its tether" by itself. In principle we are capable of every mutation, unpredictable mutations irreducible to a range or typology. Our plastic possibilities are actually never-ending.

In the usual order of things, in classical metamorphoses, transformation intervenes in place of flight. For example, when Daphne, chased by Phoebus, is unable to run fast enough, she turns into a tree. But metamorphosis by destruction is not the same as flight; it is rather the form of the impossibility of fleeing. The impossibility of flight where flight presents the only possible solution. We must allow for the impossibility of flight in situations in which an extreme tension, a pain or malaise push a person towards an outside that does not exist.

What is a way out, what can a way out be, when there is no outside, no elsewhere? These are precisely the terms used by Freud to describe the drive, that strange excitation that cannot find its release outside the psyche and that, as he writes in *Instincts and their Vicissitudes*, determines that "no actions of flight avail against them."[5] The question is how to "eliminate" the constant force of the drive. Freud writes, "What follows is an attempt at flight."[6] The verb in "what follows," literally, "*es kommt zu Bildung*," "what comes to be formed," must be taken

10

seriously here, for the verb not only announces the attempt to flee, it actually constitutes the attempt. Indeed, the only possible way out from the impossibility of flight appears to be the formation of a *form* of flight. In other words, both the formation of a type or ersatz of flight and the formation of an identity that flees itself, that flees the impossibility of fleeing itself. Identity abandoned, dissociated again, identity that does not reflect itself, does not live its own transformation, does not subjectivize its change.

Destructive plasticity enables the appearance or formation of alterity where the other is absolutely lacking. Plasticity is the form of alterity when no transcendence, flight or escape is left. The only other that exists in this circumstance is being other to the self.

It is all too true that Daphne can only escape Phoebus by transforming herself. In a sense, flight is impossible for her too. For her too, the moment of transformation is the moment of destruction: the granting and suppression of form are contemporaneous: "Her prayer was scarcely finished, when a heavy numbness seized on her limbs. Her soft breast was enveloped in a thin bark, her hair grew into foliage and her arms into branches; her foot that was just now so quick was stuck in sluggish roots, a tree top covered her face; only her radiance remained in her."[7] Nothing left of the former body other

11

than a heart that for a time beats under the bark, a few tears. The formation of a new individual is precisely this explosion of form that frees up a way out and allows the resurgence of an alterity that the pursuer cannot assimilate. In the case of Daphne, paradoxically, the being-tree nonetheless conserves, preserves, and saves the being-woman. Transformation is a form of redemption, a strange salvation, but salvation all the same. By contrast, the flight identity forged by destructive plasticity flees itself first and foremost; it knows no salvation or redemption and is there for no one, especially not for the self. It has no body of bark, no armor, no branches. In retaining the same skin, it is forever unrecognizable.

In *Le Théorème d'Almodovar*, Antoni Casas Ros describes the car accident that disfigured him: a hart appeared on the road, the writer lost control of the car, his companion died on the spot, his face was completely destroyed. "At the beginning I believed the doctors, but in the end my reconstructive surgery was unable to rid my face of its Cubism. Picasso would have hated me, for I am the negation of his invention. To think that he too would have met me at the Perpignan train station Dalí called the center of the universe. I am a blurred photograph, one that might remind you of a face."[8]

I have witnessed these types of transformation, even if they did not deform faces, even if they resulted less directly from recognizable accidents. Even if they were less spectacular, less brutal, they still had the power to start an end, to displace the meaning of a life. The couple unable to recover from an infidelity. The well-off woman whose son suddenly and inexplicably abandoned his family for a squat in the North of France. The colleague who upped and left for Texas believing he would be happy there. And in Central France, where I lived for years, all those people who at the age of 50 lost their job in the economic crisis of the mid-1980s. Teachers in underprivileged areas. People with Alzheimer's disease. In all these cases what was striking was that once the metamorphosis took place, however explicable its causes (unemployment, relational difficulties, illness), its effects were absolutely unexpected, and it became incomprehensible, displacing its cause, breaking all etiological links. All of a sudden these people became strangers to themselves because they could not flee. It was not, or not just, that they were broken, wracked with sorrow or misfortune; it was the fact that they became new people, others, re-engendered, belonging to a different species. Exactly as if they had had an accident. "An autobiography appears to be the tale of a full life. A succession of acts. The displacements of a body in space-time. Adventures, misdeeds, joys, unending suffering. My true life starts with an end."[9]

The crisis of the mid-1980s in France was a crisis of connection, a crisis that gave social exclusion its full meaning. It revolutionized the concepts of unhappiness and trauma and provoked a social upheaval whose extent we are only beginning to measure today. The jobless, the homeless, the sufferers of post-traumatic stress syndrome, the deeply depressed, the victims of natural catastrophes, all began to resemble one another as the new international whose physiognomy I tried to describe in *The New Wounded*.[10] Forms of post-traumatic subjectivity, as Žižek calls it; new figures of the void or of identitarian abandonment who elude most therapies, especially psychoanalysis.

Existing, in these cases—but, in the end, isn't it always the case?—amounts to experiencing a lack of exteriority, which is as much an absence of interiority, hence the impossible flight, the on the spot transformation. There is neither an inside nor an outside world. Consequently, the modification is all the more radical and violent; it fragments all the more readily. The worst dissensions of the subject with the self, the most serious conflicts, do not even look tragic. Paradoxically, they are signaled by indifference and coldness.

Kafka's *The Metamorphosis* is the most successful, beautiful, and relevant attempt to approach this kind of accident. Blanchot puts it well:

14

> The state in which Gregor finds himself is the same state as that of a being unable to quit existence, one for whom to exist is to be condemned to always fall back into existence. Becoming vermin, he continues to live in the mode of degeneration, he digs deeper into animal solitude, he moves closer still to absurdity and the impossibility of living. But what happens? He just keeps on living . . .[11]

Metamorphosis is existence itself, untying identity instead of reassembling it. Gregor's awakening at the beginning of the story is the perfect expression of destructive plasticity. The inexplicable nature of his transformation into an insect continues to fascinate us as a possible danger, a threat for each of us. Who knows if tomorrow . . .

But the monster does manage to weave a cocoon. A cocoon which slowly becomes a text. The text is *The Metamorphosis*, and this metamorphosis is completed by us, the readers. The circle of plastic possibilities in some senses closes here again. The narrative voice is not entirely that of an insect. This invisible butterfly has a non-bestial voice, the voice of a man, the voice of a writer. What is a metamorphosis that can still speak itself, write itself, that does not remain entirely unique even when it experiences itself as such? As Kafka writes in his letters, art is no salvation. Yet it can preserve. After all, one can't help recognizing Daphne's bark in Gregor.

If Deleuze's reading of *The Metamorphosis* is unfair when it concludes that Kafka "fails," it is not entirely wrong. On the one hand, Deleuze recognizes the effectiveness of the "becoming-animal of Gregor, his becoming beetle, junebug, dungbeetle, cockroach, which traces an intense line of flight in relation to the familial triangle but especially in relation to the bureaucratic and commercial triangle."[12] The result of the metamorphosis is precisely a being in flight, one who constitutes a way out in the self, forming "a single process, a unique method that replaces subjectivity."[13] On the other hand, Deleuze also sees "the exemplary story of a re-Oedipalization"[14] in this metamorphosis, a trajectory that remains trapped in the family triangle: father–mother–sister. "Given over to his becoming-animal, Gregor finds himself re-Oedipalized by his family and goes to his death."[15] Gregor's death returns the metamorphosis to the order of things, in some senses annulling it. The family will not have been metamorphosized and Gregor will not have stopped recognizing the family, calling, naming his father, his mother, his sister.

But Deleuze attributes the "failure" of the metamorphosis to the fact that it concerns an adventure in form, the adventure of an identifiable animal. Gregor becomes a beetle. For Deleuze, a true metamorphosis would be a metamorphosis that, despite its name, would have nothing to do with a becoming-form. According to him, "as long as there is form, there is still reterritorialization."[16] This is why the "becoming-animal" is not "becoming *an* animal": the first is an arrangement; the second is a form, which can do nothing but freeze becoming.[17]

I do not believe that the problem of the limit of metamorphoses as traditionally conceived derives from the fact that they present themselves as the journey from one form to another. It is not form that is the problem; it's the fact that form can be thought separately from the nature of the being that transforms itself. The fact that form is presented as skin, vestment or finery, and that one can always leave without an alteration in what is essential. The critique of metaphysics does not want to recognize that in fact, despite what it claims loud and clear, metaphysics constantly instigates the dissociation of essence and form, or form and the formal, as if one could always rid oneself of form, as if, in the evening, form could be left hanging like a garment on the chair of being or essence. In metaphysics, form can always change, but the nature of being persists. It is this that is debatable—not the concept of form itself, which it is absurd to pretend to do without.

We must find a way to think a mutation that engages both form and being, a new form that is literally a form of being. Again, the radical metamorphosis I am trying to think here is well and truly the fabrication of a new person, a novel form of life, without anything in common with a preceding form. Gregor changes form; we will never know what he looked like before but in some ways he remains the same, awaiting meaning. He pursues his inner monologue and does not appear to be transformed in substance, which is precisely why he suffers, since he is no longer recognized as what he never ceases to be. But imagine a Gregor perfectly indifferent to his transformation, unconcerned by it. Now that's an entirely different story!

What destructive plasticity invites us to consider is the suffering caused by an absence of suffering, in the emergence of a new form of being, a stranger to the one before. Pain that manifests as indifference to pain, impassivity, forgetting, the loss of symbolic reference points. Yet the synthesis of another soul and body in that abandonment is still a form, a whole, a system, a life. In this case the term "form" does not describe the intensity of a presence or an idea, nor that of a sculptural contour.

A very specific plastic art is at work here, one that looks a lot like the death drive. Freud knew that the death drive creates forms, which he also called "examples." However, apart from sadism and masochism, he couldn't give any examples or refer to any types. How does one render the death drive *visible*?[18]

18

2

The identity formed by brain pathologies can help us offer a response and retrospectively provide Freud with the example or type he was either missing or unwilling to see, turning his back on it as violently as he rejected his profession as a neurologist: the formation of a survivor's identity, a never before seen existential and vital configuration. A brain damaged identity which, even as an absence from the self, is nonetheless well and truly a psyche.

Advances in neurobiological research point to the need to think through a new relation of the brain—and hence also the psyche—to destruction, negativity, loss, and death.

Interestingly, some American scientists are turning to continental philosophy to develop this new relation between biology and thanatology. Antonio Damasio, for instance, recognizes a clear affinity between his work and Spinoza's philosophy. He sees Spinoza as a "proto-neurobiologist," the first philosopher to recognize the ontological, or essential, importance of the nervous system.

Damasio argues that Spinoza was also the first in the metaphysical tradition to give the concept of form a new meaning as the indissoluble identity of body and spirit. Indeed, in Part III of his *Ethics* Spinoza claims, "the first thing that constitutes the essence of the mind is simply the idea of a body that actually exists."[19] Form is thus the name given to the actual unity of body and spirit, but also, and even more deeply, to the unity of the subject's ontological constitution and biological structure.

Spinoza's achievement is not only to have accorded a fundamental role to the body but also to have inscribed biological phenomena, notably the emotions, within being itself, in other words, precisely within the fundamental ontological given that is the *conatus*, that is, the tendency of all living things to preserve their being. Damasio writes:

> The importance of biological facts in the Spinoza system cannot be overemphasized. Seen through the light of modern biology, the system is conditioned by the presence of life, the presence of a natural tendency to preserve that life; the fact that the preservation of life depends on the equilibrium of life functions and consequently on life regulation; the fact that the status of life regulation is expressed in the form of affects—joy,

sorrow—and its modulated appetites; and the fact that appetites, emotions, and the precariousness of the life condition can be known and appreciated by the human individual due to the construction of self, consciousness, and knowledge-based reason.[20]

It is impossible to comprehend the tendency of being to conserve itself without acknowledging the role of the affects in modulating the intensity of the *conatus*. Indeed, just like the appetite, the tendency to persevere is qualitatively and quantitatively variable, more or less open, more or less intense. The hunger to live is not always equal to itself: it changes, increasing or decreasing according to affects, depending on how one feels. For Spinoza, the affects manifest a range in which joy and sorrow are two opposite poles. Joy increases the power to act, increases the intensity of the *conatus*, widens its scope. Sorrow, on the other hand, dampens, diminishes and restricts this power.

"The human body can be affected in many ways by which its power of acting is increased or diminished."[21] This power coincides precisely with "the endeavor [*conatus*] by which each thing strives to persevere in its being."[22] This "endeavor" is adjustable; it can be tuned like an instrument; joy and sorrow play it like a strange moving keyboard, making it resonate or muffling its tone. Joy affirms. Sorrow diminishes. "Joy and sorrow are passions by which the power, i.e. the endeavor, of each thing to persevere in its being is increased or diminished, helped or hindered."[23]

One cannot be without being affected. This founding observation opens a new path for neurobiology in so far as it takes into account the fundamental role of emotion in cerebral life, in other words, in the unity of the organism, the complex formed by body and spirit. Reason and cognition cannot develop or exercise their functions normally if they are not supported by affects. Reasoning without desiring is not reasoning. In order to think, to want, to know, things must have a consistency, a weight, a value, otherwise emotional indifference annuls the relief, erases differences in perspective, levels everything. When reasoning is deprived of its critical power, its ability to discriminate and make a difference that proceeds from emotion and affect, then, as Damasio says, it becomes cold-blooded reasoning, and no longer reasons: "selective reduction in emotion is at least as prejudicial for rationality as excessive emotion."[24]

In emphasizing the consubstantiality of rationality and affectivity, Spinoza anticipated current neurobiological discoveries showing that consciousness and emotion are inseparable. High-level cognitive functions such as language, memory, reasoning, and attention are

22

attached to emotional processes, "especially when it comes to personal and social matters involving risk and conflict."[25] Damasio develops the hypothesis of "emotional signals," also known as "somatic-markers": in some cerebral injuries, the marker is erased and reason loses the link connecting it to life, to the desire to survive, to the *conatus.*

> This hypothesis is known as the somatic-marker hypothesis, and the patients who led me to propose it had damage to selected areas in the prefrontal region, especially in the ventral and medial sectors, and in the right parietal regions. Whether because of a stroke or head injury or a tumor which required surgical resection, damage in those regions was consistently associated with a clinical pattern I described above, i.e. a disturbance of the ability to decide advantageously in situations involving risk and conflict and a selective reduction of the ability to resonate emotionally in precisely those same situations.[26]

The patients Damasio mentions have not lost their reason strictly speaking. Usually, their intelligence is perfectly intact. But they have left reason, they have detached themselves from it, through their inability to be affected by it.

In *Un merveilleux malheur* [a marvelous misfortune] Boris Cyrulnik analyzes the cases of children who have

23

been abused or abandoned. He shows that an impoverished affective life acts as a veritable trauma and leads to serious psychomotor delays. These children become insensible, withdrawn from the world. These phenomena of coldness and indifference are characteristics of destructive plasticity, of this power of change without redemption, without teleology, without any meaning other than strangeness. The new identities of neurological patients have one point in common: suffering to various degrees from attacks to the inductive sites of emotion, they all show this often unfathomable absence. All traumatic injuries, of whatever type, provoke this behavior of one sort or another. The question is therefore how to think the void of subjectivity, the distancing of the individual who becomes an ontological refugee, intransitive (he or she is not the other *of* someone), without any correlation, genitive or origin. A new person, whose novelty is not, however, inscribed in any temporality.

Again, let me repeat that the pathology cases examined by Damasio are not instances of madness. The brain injured are not mad; they abandon even madness. How is it possible for a subject to no longer to coincide with their own essence without going mad? Isn't it time to acknowledge the existence of an element of indifference in being itself, revealed by this instance to which philosophy usually accords not the slightest ontological value: the suffering of the brain? The brain's own pain?

Let it be said that the brain has never been an object of philosophy. Granted, it plays an important role for Descartes (in *The Passions of the Soul*) and Bergson (in *Matter and Memory*), but it remains a secondary organ that receives and transmits information without enjoying the slightest symbolic autonomy. No philosopher has ever asked whether the brain as such can feel pain, experience representations, be the center of a meaningful economy. Spinoza alone appears to be the exception to the rule. As Damasio writes:

> Spinoza might have intuited the principles behind the natural mechanisms responsible for the parallel manifestations of mind and body . . . I am convinced that mental processes are grounded in the brain's mappings of the body, collections of neural patterns that portray responses to events that cause emotion and feelings. Nothing could have been more comforting than coming across this statement of Spinoza's and wondering about its possible meaning.[27]

A contemporary definition of Spinoza's *conatus* might run as follows: "It is the aggregate of dispositions laid down in brain circuitry that, once engaged by internal or environmental conditions, seeks both survival and

25

well-being."[28] The vital regulation proceeds from cerebral activity defined here as the shared work of cognition and emotion. Damasio continues:

> the large compass of activities of the *conatus* is conveyed to the brain, chemically and neurally. This is accomplished by chemical molecules transported in the bloodstream, as well as by electrochemical signals transmitted along nerve pathways. Numerous aspects of the life process can be so signaled to the brain and represented there in numerous maps made of circuits of nerve cells located in specific brain sites. By that point we have reached the treetops of life regulation, the level at which feelings begin to coalesce.[29]

The specific concept of the differentiated identity of body and spirit developed by Spinoza allows us to imagine that he understood perfectly the role of the brain, which is precisely to ensure this unity, to incarnate it, in the true sense of the word. The hypothesis of a transformability of the *conatus* that coincides with its constant affective variability, with the mutability of its tension, intensity, and tone, lays the groundwork for thinking through the damages caused by an attack on the areas of the brain that are emotion inductors. When the range of affects linked to the deployment of the *conatus* are injured or damaged, identity is profoundly altered, effectively metamorphosized.

When a trauma occurs, the entire affective potential is influenced, sorrow is not even possible any more; the patient falls, beyond sorrow, into a state of apathy that is no longer either joyful or despairing. They become indifferent to their own survival and to the survival of others. How else can we explain indifference to murder?

On December 18, 2004, Romain Dupuy, a former patient of Pau Hospital in the Pyrenees, entered the hospital by breaking through a skylight. He killed two nurses, attacking their bodies viciously and going so far as to decapitate one of them. "He did not appear to know the victims, who were killed simply because on that night they happened to be in the residence closest to where he stayed when he was there,"[30] writes the local newspaper. At the time, some patients were watching television—on which Dupuy placed the severed head before fleeing. Some of them therefore witnessed the crime without saying a word. It is difficult to know what is worse: the murders, or the indifference of the spectators who saw everything and did not react.

It might be objected that in this instance both the executioner and the spectators were psychiatric patients, and were not, strictly speaking, brain damaged. But while it is true that all psychic illness (schizophrenia is the clearest example) causes an attack on the emotional brain (particularly the frontal lobe), it is not possible to grasp the coldness of the killer or the indifference of the spectators without referring to brain injuries that cause the sometimes total and irremediable loss of emotion.

There is no need to look for extreme examples to understand to what point injuries to the emotional brain are true threats to vital regulation and hence survival:

> There is growing evidence that feelings, along with the appetites and emotions that most often cause them, play a decisive role in social behavior. . . . After the onset of their brain lesion these patients are generally not able to hold on to their premorbid social status, and all of them cease to be financially independent. They usually do not become violent, and their misbehavior does not tend to violate the law. Nonetheless, the proper governance of their lives is profoundly affected. It is apparent that, if left to their own devices, their survival with well-being would be in serious question. . . . Their spouses note a lack of empathy. The wife of one of our patients noted how her husband, who previously reacted with care and affection anytime she was upset, now reacted with indifference in the same circumstances. Patients who prior to their disease were known to be concerned with social projects in their communities or who were known for their ability to counsel friends and relatives in difficulty

28

no longer show any inclination to help. For practical purposes, they are no longer independent human beings.[31]

The individual's history is cut definitively, breached by the meaningless accident, an accident that it is impossible to re-appropriate through either speech or recollection. In principle a brain injury, a natural catastrophe, a brutal, sudden, blind event cannot be reintegrated retrospectively into experience. These types of events are pure hits, tearing and piercing subjective continuity and allowing no justification or recall in the psyche. How do you internalize a cerebral lesion? How do you speak about emotional deficit since words must be carried by the affects whose very absence is precisely what is in question here?

These questions help us draw attention to the increasing gap between classical psychoanalysis and contemporary neurobiology. This is a divorce that can and must also become a space of dialogue. What is at stake is destructive plasticity.

We must recognize, however, that neurobiologists do not develop the notion of destructive plasticity as such. Destruction lies at the heart of their analyses; the formation of a new personality resulting from this destruction is also a constant object of investigation. Yet brain injury and its consequences for identity are still treated as contingent facts, subject to chance, with no link to an existential potential for the subject. The possibility of an identity change by destruction, the possibility of an annihilating metamorphosis, does not appear as a constant virtuality of being, inscribed in it as an eventuality, understood within its biological and ontological fate. Destruction remains an accident while really, to make a pun that suggests that the accident is a property of the species, destruction should be seen as a species of accident, so that the ability to transform oneself under the effect of destruction is a possibility, an existential structure. This structural status of the identity of the accident does not, however, reduce the chance of it happening, does not annul the contingency of its occurrence, which remains absolutely unpredictable in all instances. This is why recognizing the ontology of the accident is a philosophically difficult task: it must be acknowledged as a law that is simultaneously logical and biological, but a law that does not allow us to anticipate its instances. Here is a law that is surprised by its own instances. In principle, destruction does not respond to its own necessity, and when it occurs, does not comfort its own possibility. Strictly speaking, destruction does not come to pass.

This destructive plasticity should be included in the register of cerebral laws. An identity change is not only the consequence of an external event, arising from pure chance, affecting and altering an originally stable identity. Normal identity is a changeable and transformable entity right from the start, always liable to make a *faux bond* or to say farewell to itself.

Spinoza may be able to help us again here, but in a far more radical manner than either Damasio or even Deleuze imagined. It is peculiar that neither of them really paid attention to the *Scholium* of Proposition 39 in Part Four of the *Ethics*, which states: "Those things that bring about the preservation of the ratio of motion and rest that the parts of the human body have to one another are good; on the other hand, those things are bad that bring it about that the parts of the human body have another ratio of motion and rest to one another."[32] This proposition explains the difference between life and death. Life can be defined as the harmonious agreement of the movements of the body. This is the definition of the health of the organism, assuming an accordance between its parts. On the other hand, death occurs when the parts have their own, autonomous movements, thereby disorganizing the life of the whole and breaking up its unity.

In the *Scholium* Spinoza expands on a strange and interesting remark. Having posited, "I understand the body to have died when its parts are so disposed that they maintain a different ratio of motion and rest to one another," he adds:

> For I am not so bold as to deny that the human body, whilst retaining the circulation of the blood and other features on account of which a body is thought to live, *can nevertheless be changed into another nature which is very different from its own* [emphasis mine]. For no reason compels me to assert that the body does not die unless it is turned into a corpse; indeed, experience seems to speak in favor of something else. For it happens sometimes that a man suffers such changes that it is not easy for me to say that he is the same. For example, I have heard of a certain Spanish poet who was stricken with disease, and although he recovered from it, he was so forgetful of his past life that he did not believe that the dramatic poems and tragedies that he had written were his own, and could indeed have been taken for a grown-up infant if he had not also forgotten his native language. And if this seems incredible, what shall we say of infants? A man of mature years thinks their nature to be so different from his that he could be persuaded that he was never an infant, unless he had made a conjecture about himself from the example of others. But I prefer to leave these matters undecided, rather than to provide the superstitious with material for raising new questions.[33]

32

Spinoza is referring to the poet Góngora, who in 1627 lost his memory a year before his death, and whose works Spinoza owned. In considering his case, Spinoza appears to accept a sort of death that is not death but that appears instead as a radical personality change. As if an in-between life and death existed, complicating the binary distinction introduced in Proposition 39. As if there were a partial death resulting from a mysterious metamorphosis of the body and affects, one that would not coincide with the end of the relation of movement and rest between the parts of the body, but that would proceed from the disorganization of this relation. Some parts of the body living their own lives alone become autonomous, dissolving the whole without entirely annihilating it. This is what gives the impression of madness. The writer who no longer remembers his own books, who no longer remembers himself, is dead without being dead. His "nature" is "changed into another nature which is very different from its own."[34] Let us note clearly that Spinoza does not say his "appearance" or his physical "envelope"; he says his "nature," that is, his essence, or again, his form.

This is one of the only references made in a philosophical text to a destructive metamorphosis of the nature of a being, from whence a new being, who is in some senses a living-dead, is born. The body can die without being dead. There is a destructive mutation that is not the transformation of the body into a cadaver, but rather the transformation of the body into another body in the same body, due to an accident, a lesion, an injury, or a catastrophe. We can see that for Spinoza there is a great opening in the existential possibility in which the diminished negative extreme exceeds sorrow by far, since it is a matter of a mutation of essence within essence, of something that transgresses the normal range of variations of the *conatus*. Spinoza says that even childhood appears to be a change of this sort, an originary change, a metamorphosis prior to reason, which also prevents us from thinking that the ill can fall back into childhood, since childhood is no longer the certain and solid term of regression, but rather another state of ourselves towards which it is fundamentally impossible to regress since it is not stable. We return nowhere. Between life and death we become other to ourselves.

In *Expressionism in Philosophy: Spinoza*, Deleuze lays claim to the great changeability of the *conatus* in a philosopher who is traditionally considered the thinker of strict necessity, without temporality or change. Deleuze writes: "One already senses the fundamental importance of that area of the *Ethics* that concerns existential changes of finite modes, or expressive changes."[35] These "expressive" variations, associated with the *conatus*, are of two orders.

The first, to which I have already referred, concerns the normal variations of affects between activity (joy) and passivity (sorrow): one is more or less apt to act, to exercise one's power, depending on the affects orienting one's "form," that is, the *conatus* at any given moment. Deleuze continues:

> If we manage to produce active affections, our passive affections will be correspondingly reduced. And as far as we still have passive affections, our power of action will be correspondingly "inhibited." In short, for a given essence, for a given capacity to be affected, the power of suffering and that of acting should be open to variation in inverse proportion one to the other. Both together, in their varying proportions, constitute the capacity to be affected.[36]

But some emotions appear to touch not the different nuances of the range of the *conatus*, but rather the very structure of the *conatus* and are consequently referred to as the second type of "expressive variations." Deleuze explains: "We must next introduce another level of possible variation. For the capacity to be affected does not remain fixed at all times and from all viewpoints."[37] For example, "growth, ageing, illness: we can hardly recognize the same individual. And is it really indeed the same individual? Such changes, whether imperceptible or abrupt, in the relation that characterizes a body, may also be seen in its capacity of being affected, as though the capacity and the relation enjoy a margin, a limit, within which they take form and are deformed."[38]

It is thus no longer a question here of mood variations, but of changes in the nature of the finite being experiencing these moods. Thus, illness and old age are mutations in the structure of the *conatus* itself. These structural mutations show what Deleuze calls the "elasticity" of the *conatus*: "Spinoza suggests, in fact, that the relation that characterizes an existing mode as a whole is endowed with a kind of elasticity."[39]

Is the term "elasticity" appropriate in this instance? An "elastic" material is characterized by its ability to return to its initial form without changing. But the change described here is irreversible, a return to the initial form is impossible. The word we need is "plasticity," which refers precisely to this power of modification of the identity in proportions that exceed the simple detour or hiccup. The examples given by Deleuze (old age, serious illness) exceed the concept he uses to designate them.

For Spinoza there is therefore a tendency for the finite mode to de-subjectivize. In the work of this thinker who,

I repeat, is viewed as the enemy of freedom, there is in fact a recognition of an ontological plasticity that is both positive—the plasticity of the affects—and negative—the absolute modification of the mode, the production of another existence unrelated to the previous existence.

The changes brought about by destructive plasticity result from the divergence in the movements that constitute the changes, the disorder of its directions. In contemporary neurology coldness, neutrality, absence, a "flat" emotional state, are instances of this mode of destructive plasticity that Spinoza anticipated by envisaging the existence of a destructive metamorphic power, without any possible reintegration into the thread of a life, a fate or a true idea.

Acknowledgement of the role of destructive plasticity allows us to radicalize the deconstruction of subjectivity, to stamp it anew. This recognition reveals that a power of annihilation hides within the very constitution of identity, a virtual coldness that is not only the fate of the brain injured, schizophrenics, and serial killers, but is also the signature of a law of being that always appears to be on the point of abandoning itself, escaping. An ontology of modification must shelter this particular type of metamorphosis that is a farewell to being itself. A farewell that is not death, a farewell that occurs within life, just like the indifference of life to life by which survival sometimes manifests itself. Today we see that all trauma survivors, whether of biological or political trauma, show signs of this kind of indifference. In this sense, we must take destructive brain plasticity into account as a hermeneutic tool to understand the contemporary faces of violence.

"You are your synapses."[40] Joseph LeDoux's famous phrase would thus not only mean an assimilation of the being of the subject to the constructive plastic formation of their identity, but also the identification of being as the possibility of its own neuronal destructive plasticity.

The inscription of a death drive in the brain as an emotional coldness is thus not only visible among those with brain injuries, schizophrenics, serial killers, trauma victims and all the other figures of social exclusion; it is also potentially present as a threat in each one of us. Contemporary neurobiological discourse would benefit from a more radical meditation on Spinoza's formulation that "no one has so far determined what the body can do."[41]

3

Let us take time now to consider a difficulty in Deleuze's reading of Spinoza. How and why should old age and illness be treated together? Isn't one gradual and natural while the other is always unexpected, sudden, scandalous? How can these identity changes be considered as deriving from the same register, namely the plasticity of the *conatus*?

The problem of ageing is widely characterized as a loss of plasticity. Here again we are talking about a loss of "good" plasticity. It does not occur to anyone that another plasticity might be at work when the "good" plasticity leaves the scene. It seems that two competing conceptions of ageing counter one another obscurely, inviting us to re-examine, in the light of both creative and destructive plasticity, the definition of ageing as *change* and thereby to understand how ageing can be subsumed to illness as event.

The first, most widespread conception of ageing, both in general opinion and in the scientific community, is a teleological concept in which ageing is the natural end of life, the decline that necessarily follows maturity. It appears that ageing is inconceivable apart from the gradual movement of "becoming-old." The most obvious image of this kind of becoming is the one proposed by psychoanalyst Gérard Le Gouès, a clinical specialist of the older subject, in his book *L'Âge et le principe de plaisir* [Age and the Pleasure Principle], in which he compares life to an airplane journey: "We have all flown in an airplane. Most of us know . . . that a flight can be broken down into roughly three parts: *take off*, *cruising*, and *descent*. If we understand childhood and youth as take off and adulthood as cruising, then the descent might be seen to represent the time it takes to land."[42] Ageing would therefore be equivalent to starting the descent: "To return to the aviation image, we have already seen that ageing can be compared to the descent of a flight, experienced passively by a subject who views themselves in terms of biological determinism as a passenger on a commercial flight, or lived actively, if the subject decides to take matters into their own hands, in the same way that a pilot controls the commands."[43] The metaphor of a flight certainly characterizes ageing as a slow and gradual process that starts at mid-life and which, without necessarily being linear or without turbulence, nevertheless proceeds through an orderly traversing of subsequent stages.

40

According to the schema of becoming-old, to be plastic is to know how to give form to decline gradually, in some senses, to invent one's old age, to know how to "manage it," to "remain young." By contrast, a loss of plasticity is seen as the acceptance of the descent, withdrawal, passivity or pure receptivity of the final destruction or explosion, without any means of creating a form.

A second conception defines ageing not just as a gradual process but also, and differently, as an event. A sudden rupture or flight crash, if you like. Even in the most peaceful ageing there will always be an accidental, catastrophic dimension. This concept of accident-ageing complicates the first schema. It teaches us that, in order to age, becoming-old is in some ways insufficient. Something else is needed, namely, the event of ageing. Sudden, unpredictable, upsetting everything all at once. This concept of ageing can no longer be termed becoming-old, but rather "the instantaneity of ageing," if we are willing to understand this as an unexpected, sudden metamorphosis, like the ones we sometimes read about: "her hair went white overnight." Something happens that precipitates the subject into old age, imprinting a collapse on becoming-old that both is, and is not, its realization. A stupid accident, a piece of bad news, mourning, pain—and abruptly becoming freezes, creating an unprecedented being, form, individual.

This is how it is for both ageing and death: instantaneity renders the limit between the natural and the accidental undecidable. Do we age naturally or violently? Do we die naturally or violently? Isn't death always either all one—or all the other?

Do we ever really notice those around us becoming old? We notice a few wrinkles, a few sags, a few lapses. But even so, there's always one fine day when we no longer say "he or she is ageing" but rather "he's old, she's old," he or she has metamorphosized into an old person like in some tragic version of a childhood fairy tale. From the perspective of this second conception, plasticity characterizes an explosive transformation of the individual, a pure rupture. Old age is an existential break—not a continuity.

The reader might wish to stop me at this point to argue that what usually separates these two concepts of ageing is simply the intervention of pathology. On the airplane's descent, the pathological accident that interrupts becoming and introduces the event-dimension of metamorphosis may intervene during the natural process of ageing. But it is not, or in any case not only, the arrival of illness that allows us to separate the two concepts of ageing. Indeed, the same illness, even the same lesion, can be interpreted in terms of both the continuity schema and the event schema. Illness can just as well be considered the fulfillment of a fate as a rupture. In this sense Deleuze is right to place possibilities of old age and illness on the same existential plane. On these grounds I agree that both conceptions of ageing can characterize any type of ageing subject, in good or poor health. Only if we are willing to forge paradigms for thinking old age out of these two conceptions can we really attempt a satisfying approach to the mental pathology of the older subject and, consequently, to late treatment.

The first concept of ageing, becoming-old, is governed by a certain understanding of plasticity that was essentially developed by classical psychoanalysis. Freud's use of the concept of "plasticity" (*Plastizität*) is very suggestive. He endows the term with two fundamental meanings. First there is what he calls the "plasticity of psychic life," which refers to the indestructible nature of the traces that make up the psychic fate of the subject. We know that for Freud no experience is forgotten. The trace is indelible. The trace can be modified, deformed, reformed—but never erased. The primitive does not disappear. Thus, in psychic life:

> every earlier stage of development persists alongside the later stage which has arisen from it; here succession also involves co-existence although it is to the same materials that the whole series of transformations has applied. The

43

earlier mental state may not have manifested itself for years, but none the less it is so far present that it may at any time again become the mode of expression of the forces in the mind, and indeed the only one, as though all later developments had been annulled or undone. This extraordinary plasticity of mental developments is not unrestricted as regards direction; it may be described as a special capacity for involution—for regression— since it may well happen that a later and higher stage of development, once abandoned, cannot be reached again. But the primitive stages can always be re-established; the primitive mind is, in the fullest meaning of the word, imperishable. What are called mental diseases inevitably produce an impression in the layman that intellectual and spiritual life have been destroyed. In reality, the destruction only applies to later acquisitions and developments. The essence of mental disease lies in a return to earlier states of affective life and of functioning. An excellent example of the plasticity of mental life is afforded by the state of sleep, which is our goal every night. Since we have learnt to interpret even absurd and confused dreams, we know that whenever we go to sleep we throw off our hard-won morality like a garment, and put it on again next morning.[44]

Plasticity thus refers to the possibility of being transformed without being destroyed; it characterizes the entire strategy of modification that seeks to avoid the threat of destruction.

The second Freudian definition of plasticity concerns the vitality of the libido. The plasticity of the libido is related to its mobility (*Bewegtheit*), in other words, its ability to change its object, not to remain fixed, the capacity to change its investments. Sexual and amorous energy invest an object, but do not oblige the subject to hang on to the object forever; the subject must retain a degree of suppleness, plasticity, in order to be able to attach itself to another object, in other words, to remain free.

The effectiveness of the analytic cure depends primarily on this libidinal plasticity. The patient must be able to evolve, to give up former investments, to construct new links in their place, to desire differently. The plasticity of the libido enables the patient not to remain a prisoner to a fixed psychic configuration that is usually paralyzing and painful.

Yet Freud characterizes ageing precisely as a loss of, or notable reduction in, this plasticity of the libido in so far as sexual investment weakens. In "The Wolf Man," he states: "We only know one thing about them, and that is that mobility of the mental cathexes is a quality which shows striking diminution with the advance of age."[45] Over time, as a result of this erotic weakening, the patient can no longer begin an analysis. Healing the mental problems of older people would thus be a lost cause.

Today, the verdict is less damning and the possibility of late treatment is clearly supported and implemented. In *L'Âge et le principe de plaisir*, Le Gouès returns to Freud's dual articulation of the concept of plasticity, namely, the indestructibility of psychic life and the tenacity of libidinal investments. He demonstrates that the ageing subject tries to compensate for the natural weakening of libidinal investments through an unconscious emphasis on psychic life, marked by a return to infantile psychic forms. Supposedly the older person returns to the solipsism and egotism of the child. Libidinal weakening is accompanied by a reinforcement of the partial pre-genital drives and a narcissistic withdrawal. Ferenczi too noticed this, as he explains: "Older people become child-like again, narcissistic, losing many of their family and social interests, they lack a large part of their ability to sublimate . . . Their libido regresses to the pregenital stages of development."[46]

Le Gouès does not adopt the vision of an ageing-event or instantaneous ageing. He writes:

One cannot give an exact date for the beginning of psychic ageing since it is not an event, like birth, but rather a slow, gradual process similar to the process of

46

growing, in some ways the direct opposite of growing. Nevertheless, it can be assigned a psychic beginning since this ageing begins the moment that the fantasy of eternity meets a previously forgotten limit of the libido, when this fantasy is upset by the appearance of an enduring flagging—whether it is in a loss of seduction in the woman or a diminishment of energy in the man—a flagging with many affective, mental, bodily, professional and social consequences.[47]

Le Gouès recognizes the existence of a "psychic beginning" to ageing, but this beginning is undetermined, imprecise, and derives from the "natural" slope of life, not from an accident that acts as a counterpoint to the incline.

This very conventional, classic definition of ageing, which measures it solely in terms of the loss of sexual power ("femininity" or "virility"), a loss that is both physical and psychic, genital and psychological, assumes that decline is lived in a continuous mode as a descending slope, without any abrupt event or rupture, without variation, as if the *conatus* suddenly goes dumb. Narcissistic overcompensation would ultimately supplement the genital decline: old people love themselves because they can no longer love.

To heal the older subject's difficulties would thus involve an attempt to find new avenues for sublimation, to redevelop a depressive position or rebalance the libidi-nal equilibrium. According to this schema, plasticity refers precisely to the indestructible, to something that can be damaged or destroyed, but which never disappears entirely. To heal would inevitably amount to getting support, one way or another, from this remainder, from the shreds of childhood.

Yet are we certain that psychic life resists destruction as Freud claims? Are we certain that there is something indestructible in the psyche? Are we certain that childhood remains? Is the claim that "the essence of mental disease lies in a return to earlier states of affective life and of functioning"[48] always true? What I have termed here "the instantaneity of ageing," the possibility of changing "all of a sudden," challenges this continuity and upsets traditional definitions of old age as plasticity. The instantaneity of ageing would be that sudden event, linked to the permanent disappearance of our childhood and thus to the impossibility of taking refuge in the past, the impossibility of regression.

From a neurobiological point of view, old age is characterized by the cerebral reorganization it implies as a metamorphosis or change of identity. As Joseph LeDoux argues, "when connections change, personality, too, can change."[49] The metamorphoses that arise thus cause a deep restructuring of self-image, which leads the subject into another vital adventure, against which there is no defense or compensation.

We have seen that illness should not be considered the element that enables us to distinguish between becoming-old and the instantaneity of old age, between the gradual and the accidental concepts of ageing. Generalizing from the lessons neurobiologists have drawn from studying brain lesions, I would like to hazard that ageing itself may be thought of as a lesion. In the end it may be that for each one of us, ageing arises all of a sudden, in an instant, like a trauma, and that it suddenly transforms us, without warning, into an unknown subject. A subject who no longer has a childhood and whose fate is to live a worn-out future.

When subjects suffering from senile dementia start talking and mentioning moments in their past, who can say whether they are doing so because a liberation of the repressed dictates—in which case their words would be revelatory—or if they are saying something entirely other in a total breach with the person they once were, thereby constructing some sort of artificial story, an imposture?

The concept of accidental ageing certainly calls for a different treatment from the one used in psychoanalysis. It would require listening to, or healing, older subjects the same way that emergency rescue teams respond to an explosion or attack. Listening to or healing older subjects as if they were trauma victims.

Certainly, as Le Gouès rightly says, "there is a psychopathology suited to the individual, according to his or her prior personality, according to his or her ability or inability to withstand the experiences of strangeness that are inflicted on the person by the brain injury."[50] The two types of ageing—progressive and instantaneous—are always intertwined and implicated in one another, and no doubt someone will object that some part of the deteriorated identity will always remain, that part of the structure of the personality will persist beyond changes. But even so, how many people leave us and leave themselves before they disappear entirely?

*

The passage in Marcel Proust's *Finding Time Again* in which the aged narrator revisits his former acquaintances after many years absence, at the "gathering" thrown at the Guermantes' mansion, is an extraordinary staging of the two concepts of ageing discussed here, the becoming-old and instantaneous old age. Proust essentially makes the two coincide. More precisely, having prepared this moment throughout *In Search of Lost Time*, he brings them into conflict, running them up against each other, in the secret of a vertiginous and angst-ridden unity.

The guests have become unrecognizable. "To begin with," says the narrator "I did not understand why I was so slow to recognize the master of the house and the guests nor why everybody seemed to have put on make-up, in most cases with powdered hair which changed them completely."[51] This "which changed them completely" is critical, for it reveals a divided, conflictual transformation, simultaneous continuity and rupture.

Initially, it seems that the "distorting perspective of Time"[52]—the point of view that undoes form, strictly speaking—corresponds merely to the passing of the years and produces the sculpting of a being who has certainly changed in appearance but who remains, essentially, the same. A person who has "become old," wearing the accessories added by time: wrinkles, some sagging, a white beard, a hunched back, a thickened silhouette, a loss of transparence and elasticity of the skin. . . These strange, indefinable things, like the "trace of verdigris" on Madame de Guermantes' cheeks: "In the cheeks of the Duchesse de Guermantes, still very recognizable but now as variegated as nougat, I could make out a trace of verdigris, a small pink patch of crushed shell, and a little lump, hard to define, smaller than a mistletoe berry and less transparent than a glass pearl."[53]

On the one hand, the composition of the new individual appears to have been effected without a hitch, the end of a gradual movement, an incessant and smooth staging, as if time were superposed on the subject: "He [Time] is also an artist who works extremely slowly. That replica of Odette's face, for example, the first outline sketch for which I had glimpsed in Gilberte's face on the day I saw Bergotte for the first time, Time had now finally taken to the most perfect likeness, in the same way that some painters keep a work for a long time, finishing it gradually, year by year."[54] Here is the long labor, the constitutive deformation of becoming-old, starting with the replacement of each cell by another and slowly preparing, in each of us, our final annihilation.

The characters appear to have disguised themselves, as if they were acting. They have donned hairpieces and wigs and have altered the form of their bodies with cushions, strange and artificial rolls of flesh. The paradox of ageing is that it looks like a theatrical make-over, developing costume art to fabricate the most natural of states. Transvestitism is the best ally of becoming-old, its face and complicit hand-maid.

But even this metaphor of transvestitism renders the interpretation of ageing more complex. If transvestitism is necessary, it is because old age remains fundamentally a rupture; it breaks being at an unlocatable point, forcing it to change direction, leading it to become other, as one changes oneself. The old people in Proust's scenario are both disguised as what they are and transformed into entirely different characters. They are both tracking shots of themselves and snapshots of an absolute metamorphosis. "The facial features, if they change, if they form a different ensemble . . . take on a different meaning with their different appearance,"[55] writes Proust. The deformed portraits "were not likenesses."[56] Monsieur d'Argencourt's eye appears to be sculpted in a material "so changed" from what it was in times past "that the expression itself became quite different and even appeared to belong to a different person." Proust adds: "he had contrived to look so different from himself that I had the illusion of being in the presence of another person altogether."[57]

Elsewhere we come across this striking passage: "Taken to this extreme, the art of disguise becomes something more than that, it becomes a complete transformation of the personality." D'Argencourt, "with nothing but his own body to work with, had become so different from himself"! How can we not recall here Spinoza's analysis discussed above: "sometimes . . . it is not easy for me to say that he is the same"?[58] Are we not also witness here to this mutation not of the range of the *conatus* but of its very structure, pushing it to the most radical transformation? "This was evidently the furthest extremity to which he had been able to bring it [his body] without its collapsing entirely."[59] This type of spectacle "seemed to extend the possibilities available for the transformation of the human body."[60]

How can we imagine this beyond the limits of transformation except as the work of destructive plasticity, which sculpts by annihilating precisely at the point where the repertory of viable forms has reached exhaustion and has nothing else to propose?

As a result of its ambiguity—both an excess of self and a brusque incognito—old age is in no way a work of truth. Between gradual becoming and instantaneous precipitate, it never reveals the "true" nature of beings, a nature which would show itself "in the end," even if, through the gradual deformation mentioned earlier, like the work of an artist, it does accentuate the salient features of the individual. Old age eludes truth, eludes its own truth, its own power of revelation. What it reveals is just as much the *self*, the being identical to itself, as the *other*, the entirely metamorphosized being. Proust highlights this plastic ambiguity of time endlessly. The progression, evolution, inflection, repetition, but also the instantaneous, the infinitely rapid, the bump, the accident, which appears to elude duration, or at least to introduce into the thickness of succession the undatable bifurcation of destruction, sharp as a claw, unpredictable, throbbing, magnificent.

4

Because of the rhythmic and ontological ambivalence of time, another possibility for ageing is ageing before ageing. Something happens early on that precipitates the subject into a radical eclipse of youth, stealing youth away by condemning her to follow an unmarked, unpredictable track, taking her on the adventure of a sudden and tragic metamorphosis that tears her away from youth in the flower of her younger years.

In *The Lover*, Marguerite Duras describes herself exactly as an "aged girl," a woman aged by accident, too soon, subjected to destructive plasticity.

It begins in the very first lines with her face. It all starts with an encounter with a man at an airport. The man says to her: "I've known you for years. Everyone says you were beautiful when you were young, but I want to tell you I think you're more beautiful now than then. Rather than your face as a young woman, I prefer your face as it is now. Ravaged."[61]

Is there anyone who is not surprised by the photographs of the young Marguerite Duras? Did we not all ask how such a pretty girl could have transformed herself into that shrunken, toady, raspy voiced woman with her chunky glasses and cigarette hanging from thick lips? The transformation did not in fact occur over the years, as one might have imagined; it was well and truly instantaneous. Suddenly, right in the midst of her youth, the first woman brutally became the second. Duras was young for only a very short time, just eighteen years. Like Gregor Samsa in *The Metamorphosis*, she woke up metamorphosized. No one was ever able to see the transition. Between the photograph of the pretty young girl and images of the writer there is no intermediary, which is no doubt why we are so surprised, incredulous. Duras seems to have been preserved from, deprived of, the gradual erosion of time, the first aspect of deformation described by Proust. She appears to have been thrown ahead of herself by a secret anticipatory device:

> Very early in my life it was too late. It was already too late when I was eighteen. Between eighteen and twenty-five my face took off in a new direction. I grew old at eighteen. I don't know if it's the same for everyone. I've never asked. But I believe I've heard of the way time can suddenly accelerate on people when they're going through even the most youthful and highly esteemed stages of life. My ageing was very sudden. I saw it spread over my features one by one, changing the relationship

between them, making the eyes larger, the expression sadder, the mouth more final, leaving great creases in the forehead. But instead of being dismayed I watched this process with the same sort of interest I might have taken in the reading of a book. And I knew I was right, that one day it would slow down and take its normal course. The people who knew me at seventeen, when I went to France, were surprised when they saw me again two years later, at nineteen. And I've kept it ever since, the new face I had then. It has been my face. It's got older still, of course, but less, comparatively, than it would otherwise have done. It's scored with deep, dry wrinkles, the skin is cracked. But my face hasn't collapsed, as some with fine features have done. It's kept the same contours, but its substance has been laid waste. I have a face laid waste.[62]

Here then two ageings are superimposed, the "normal" second ageing of becoming, moving more slowly than the other and never entirely catching up with it, acting on damage already done, an ageing following the way "time can suddenly accelerate," the after-instantaneousness. Twice Duras grew old. Early and late.

The slap on the face of the young girl is simply of the order of the pure event, without cause or explanation. The scar on Marguerite's face can certainly be explained. Marguerite Duras, who was then Marguerite Donadieu, had a very sad and unhappy childhood. Her father died when she was only seven. Her brother Pierre, an opium addict, subjected her to verbal and sexual abuse. She argued constantly with her mother, who was manic depressive and never hid her preference for her son.

Duras began to drink in Indochina. Early indicators of her drink habit can be seen in *The Sea Wall*, when Suzanne gradually takes a liking to the taste of the champagne offered by Mr. Jo. "I became an alcoholic as soon as I started to drink,"[63] Duras later wrote. So yes, the scar across Marguerite's face can be explained—but as an anticipation, a premonition, of the alcoholism to come.

> Now I see that when I was very young, eighteen, fifteen, I already had a face that foretold the one I acquired through drink in middle age. Drink accomplished what God did not. It also served to kill me; to kill. I acquired that drinker's face before I drank. Drink only confirmed it. The space for it existed in me. I knew it the same as other people, but, strangely, in advance. Just as the space existed in me for desire. At the age of fifteen I had the face of pleasure, and yet I had no knowledge of pleasure. There was no mistaking that face. Even my mother must have seen it. My brothers did. That was how everything started for me—with that flagrant, exhausted face, those rings round the eyes, in advance of time and experience.[64]

58

Experience. True: here the accident is the experiential dimension of ontology.

The unexpected direction the face takes is also the annunciatory sign of the coldness forever separating before and after. Coldness and indifference. Sometimes, in some cases, one fine day a person no longer loves their parents and family. "Now I don't love them anymore. I don't remember if I ever did. I've left them."[65] This kind of disenchantment does not come "with" time either. One does not gradually stop loving one's family. Perhaps one never "gradually" stops loving anyone at all. I'm tempted to say that the end of love is always brutal. But in the case of family, certainly, it happens all of a sudden, like a death. One takes one's leave of them before death, so that the real death only confirms the spiritual death. But it hurts all the same. It is empty and cold and very scary to say farewell before the end, to say farewell forever when nothing is permanent yet.

Yes, the scar across Marguerite's face can be explained. But alcohol is not the cause, since that too comes later. Actually, there is no cause, which is no doubt why Duras says that God does not exist and that he can only be replaced by alcohol. "What they lack is a god. The void you discover one day in your teens—nothing can ever undo that discovery. But alcohol was invented to help us bear the void in the universe—the motion of the planets, their imperturbable wheeling through space, their silent indifference to the place of our pain. A man who drinks is interplanetary. He moves through interstellar space."[66]

But this sidereal way of being arrives brutally, from another planet, without cause, and is absolutely tyrannical in its lack of reason. Duras repeats: "I became an alcoholic as soon as I started to drink."[67] The incredible coincidence of the beginning and becoming—as soon as I began / I became—is terrifying. "I drank like one straight away."[68] All of a sudden, habitually. A habit from the first time. "[I] left everyone else behind. I began by drinking in the evening, then at midday, then in the morning, and then I began to drink at night. First once a night, then every two hours. I've never drugged myself any other way. I've always known that if I took to heroin it would soon get out of control."[69]

Alcoholism can be explained by its sudden emergence. In other words, it has no explanation. The sailor from Gibraltar leaves everything—work, family, everyone he knows, his "network"—for no reason, to live a wandering love with a woman on a boat. They both drink constantly.

> I drank whisky to restore myself. I was drinking more and more of it. So was she. We both drank more and

more as the voyage went on. First of all in the evening. Then in the afternoon as well. Then in the morning. Every day we started a bit earlier. There was always some whisky on board. She'd been drinking it for a long time, of course, ever since she'd been looking for him, but during this voyage I think she drank it with more pleasure than before. I soon got into her rhythm of drinking, and completely gave up trying to restrain her when we were together.[70]

We never know the reason for this wandering, which is its own context, detached from everything, riding on the sea, alone.

Duras' style is based entirely on suppressing links and causal connections, on the rhetorical figure known as asyndeton. An asyndeton is a sort of ellipse in which the conjunctions that combine the propositions and segments of the sentence are removed. It is defined as a "figure obtained through the suppression of connective terms."[71] It belongs to the class of disjunctions and it telescopes words, which come one after the other, one on top of the other, occurring as what amounts to so many accidents. They dent each another, lose all flexibility, surface, grease, society. The asyndeton is linguistic alcoholism.

Use of asyndeton may cause interpretative difficulties, confusion. This rhetorical figure removes any conjunctions whatsoever from the sentence: the copula (the verb to be), chronological conjunctions (before, after), logical conjunctions (but, for, thus), deictics and adverbs. The main effect is an expression of disorder, which is why the asyndeton is frequently used in dialogues to convey a speaker's confusion: "I'm dead tired, beat, worn out, exhausted."[72]

Duras does not seek to establish causalities; she offers mechanical sequences which appear to have no connection to one another, fortuitous: "She straightened up, slowly, as if she were being raised, and adjusted her coat again. He didn't help her. She still sat facing him, saying nothing. The first men came in, were surprised, gave the patronne a questioning look."[73]

Repetition and enumeration—nouns, participles, verbs—are also characteristic of Duras' writing style. Repetition scatters, disseminates: "he did whatever Ma took it in her head to have done—he paved, planted, transplanted, trimmed, dug out, replanted all she liked."[74] "The mother grew grim, silent, jealous."[75] "On the fifteen land concessions of the plain of Kam, they had settled, ruined, driven off, resettled and again ruined and driven off perhaps a hundred families."[76]

And then there's the phrasal verb, throwing the verb or main proposition to the end of the sentence: "Jealous. Jealous she is."[77] "And make so many detours to catch up with her, that he could never do."[78] "Shameless, that's what we were."[79]

There's also the noun left to the end of the sentence: "We'd figure it out so it'd make us happy, money."[80] Or: "I often bracket my two brothers together as she used to do, our mother."[81] "We're together, she and us, her children."[82] "Death, a chain reaction of death, started with him, the child."[83]

The subject no longer moves in the direction of becoming, the subject is no longer placed on the incline that, in the usual downhill sequence, connects substance to copula and to predicates or accidents. The subject finds herself at the end, as if emerging from her accidents, from her own destruction, which has no meaning and comes out of nowhere. The old age that arises so rapidly in the writer, scarring her face, again comes out of nowhere, is preceded by nothing, is the trace of no childhood, since childhood is like a mirage without duration or substance. "It's soon too late in life."[84]

This kind of ageing, the ageing when "time can suddenly accelerate," is not the ageing that killed Duras, who died at 82, in other words, old, in the end resisting alcohol and illness in spite of all expectations. She didn't die of her first ageing. The second ageing ultimately created the ineluctable necessity of the first ageing. Duras did not die of the old age of her youth.

5

While dying is natural, death nonetheless has yet to occur, it has to come, to find its possibility, and this possibility can only be accidental. Illness, collapse, malaise. Even someone who dies in their sleep does not die naturally. Death is dual: biological, logical. Unexpected too, accidental, creating its own form. An irregularity must occur for the form of death to be created there, in an improbable time that separates becoming from its own end. The time of a surreptitious invention, usually seen by no one. This interval of dead-living, in which being improvises on itself, arises anew for as long as it takes to finish it off. Being for death must eventually invent itself, make itself at the last moment, so that death, which is possible at every moment, finally becomes possible.

In *Buddenbrooks*, Thomas Mann describes the slow decline of a grand bourgeois lineage, the degeneration of four generations of merchants, consuls, and senators in the Hanseatic free town of Lübeck. But the penultimate and eponymous main character of the novel Thomas dies brutally in his prime. The suddenness of his death distinguishes it from the movement of slow degeneration that exhausts his lineage little by little. Thomas Buddenbrook dies of a simple toothache. He goes to see Herr Brecht, the family dentist, for a molar cavity. The tale of his visit heralds the painful absurdity of the death soon to come:

> It lasted three or four seconds. Herr Brecht's nervous exertions communicated themselves to Thomas Buddenbrook's whole body, he was even lifted up a little on his chair, and he heard a soft, squeaking noise coming from the dentist's throat. Suddenly there was a fearful blow, a violent shaking as if his neck were broken, accompanied by a quick cracking, crackling noise. The pressure was gone, but his head buzzed, the pain throbbed madly in the inflamed and ill-used jaw; and he had the clearest impression that the thing had not been successful: that the extraction of the tooth was not the solution of the difficulty, but merely a premature catastrophe which only made matters worse.
>
> Herr Brecht had retreated. He was leaning against his instrument-cupboard, and he looked like death. He said: "The crown—I thought so."
>
> Thomas Buddenbrook spat a little blood into the blue basin at his side, for the gum was lacerated. He asked, half-dazed: "What did you think? What about the crown?"

"The crown broke off, Herr Senator. I was afraid of it.—The tooth was in very bad condition. But it was my duty to make the experiment."

"What next?"

"Leave it to me, Herr Senator."

"What will you have to do now?"

"Take out the roots. With a lever. There are four of them."

"Four. Then you must take hold and lift four times"

"Yes—unfortunately . . . It will be perfectly agreeable to me, Herr Senator, if you come in to-morrow or next day, at whatever hour you like." . . .

With the lever—yes, yes, that was to-morrow. What should he do now? Go home and rest, sleep, if he could. . . . He got as far as Fisher's Lane and began to descend the left-hand sidewalk. After twenty paces he felt nauseated.

"I'll go over to the public house and take a drink of brandy," he thought, and began to cross the road. But just as he reached the middle, something happened to him. It was precisely as if his brain was seized and swung around, faster and faster, in circles that grew smaller and smaller, until it crashed with enormous, brutal, pitiless force against a stony center. He performed a half-turn, fell, and struck the wet pavement, his arms outstretched.

As the street ran steeply down hill, his body lay much lower than his feet. He fell upon his face, beneath which, presently, a little pool of blood began to form. His hat rolled a little way off down the road; his fur coat was wet with mud and slush; his hands, in their white kid gloves, lay outstretched in a puddle.

Thus he lay, and thus he remained, until some people came down the street and turned him over.[85]

Thomas' death comes briefly before the death of his son Hanno, the last male in the lineage and the only descendant, killed by typhoid disease. The full power of the end of the novel derives from the separation between the two deaths. One is sudden, the other slow and gradual, yet both are indicators of the same decadence. What remains is the incomprehensible, unacceptable difference between the two deaths: Thomas' sister apparently understands that one can die of typhus, but not of a toothache.

"Senator Buddenbrook had died of a bad tooth. So it was said in the town. But goodness, people don't die of a bad tooth! He had had a toothache; Herr Brecht had broken off the crown; and thereupon the Senator had simply fallen in the street. Was ever the like heard?"[86]

Thomas' death marks a pause in the unveiling of the ineluctable, slow, imperceptible and inevitable decline of the Buddenbrooks. The absurd incident at the dentist's office is the fatal detour, the underside of the other fate—the discontinuity of the accident in contrast to the unfolding of the tragedy that in principle no surprise ought to have interrupted. Conversely, Hanno is the victim of implacable tragic necessity. His effeminate and doleful character, his exacerbated musical compositions that are skillful but without true relief or form, his own chronic dental pains, settled in him like a harried fever, the evil which in the end gets the better of him, all this forms a strange counterpoint to Thomas' death. Between the decease of the father and that of the son, the conflict of instantaneity and becoming plays out.

One day, with the stroke of a pen, Hanno crosses through the last page of the precious book in which the family's genealogy is recorded. He thereby symbolically annuls the possibility of any descendants, deleting the page, right across, with two sharp, clear stokes. In this dying fire, the slow consumption of the Buddenbrook family, lit by the dim glow of lamps, the golds of Dantzig liqueur and the yellow pallor of almond paste, the accidental, stupid, unpredictable, unworthy end of Thomas is ejected like a cry. Decadence has two rhythms, two melodies, the first a slow waltz, the second dissonant and quick, the plastic creation of the lightening bolt.

*

All illnesses may be identical, but the sick are not: "In fact, there is no more resemblance between two sick people than between any two individuals."[87] Illnesses are usually considered intermediary events between life and death. But the transformation of the event of illness into a deadly event requires an event of the event. Again, this event of the event is the form of death, this apparition that depends on nothing, that is suspended in time and whose dynamic is one of pure acceleration. The form of death rushes. Often, this rush, in the figure, contour, shape adopted by the person about to die, is too fleeting to be noticed. Yet, among those who appear to us as living dead, those whose subjectivity left before time and who take on the new form of their end, for the people I discuss here, the form of death is visible, it has time, it leaps out at you. This form can be seen in emergency shelters, old people's homes, hospices for the elderly, and neurodegenerative disease treatment centers. The form of death can be defined as a sudden accommodation of the worst.

Even among those who live their lives without any serious problems, without any existential or health difficulties, the last moment is always a metamorphosis produced by destructive plasticity. One does not die as one is; one dies as one suddenly becomes. And what one becomes is always in the order of a desertion, a withdrawal that takes form.

What happened with Marguerite Duras, with the sudden collapse of her face, the precocious ageing, this accident of life and plastic, may also occur, secretly and to differing degrees and in different ways, in each of us. We form ourselves to death. And contrary to what philosophers would have us believe, this does not mean that we prepare ourselves for it, that we conceive of our death as a work, that we shape our finitude. For that which forms when one forms one's death, is death. The formal explosion prevents, warns against any discipline of death, the "watching over the soul by itself" that Socrates discussed while in prison.

If we lose all relation to childhood and the past the moment we are formed by destruction, what do we look like? What does the face we adopt at the last moment, or before, if the last moment precedes the last moment, look like? What do we look like once we are metamorphosized by destruction, once we are formed by destructive, explosive, nuclear plasticity? How do we look? However beautiful and decisive, we have rejected the figures of trees, animals, and the fantastic beings described by Ovid. We no longer look like anything living, but nor do we look like anything inanimate. We must imagine something between the animate and the inanimate, something that is not animal but that has none of the inertia of stone either. The inanimal? A between, or an instance that in no way resembles any intermediary, one that explodes mediations, outside the soul, outside the organic. A mode of being that is not even the one the death drive pushes us towards, that inorganic state of passivity, the inertia of matter.

So what are we like then? You could say: "nothing," but what does "looking like nothing" mean? People with Alzheimer's disease in oversized, borrowed hospital garb picked out of a shared stock, do they look like nothing? No. They do not look like nothing because "nothing" is a word that still resembles itself too much. It is one of those ontological inventions that says being backwards, and that consequently speaks of a way of coinciding that, even paradoxically, participates again in identity. Actually, ill people look like less than nothing.

I wonder if the way one looks, what one looks like in this moment, is the way other people look when they learn that you are no longer there, a look that more often than not is a look of indifference. You have to imagine the possibility of reading your own obituary. You look like those people, those people who don't care. It is the look they have when they read or hear the news, that look of mild surprise, the slight frown, the very brief pause, a few memories, five minutes of eyes unfocused. It is the indifference to the death of the other that composes the face of all those subjects who are absent from themselves. Impassivity that freezes until it never again makes a difference.

I really think that is how we look. We anticipate not death, but the indifference of others to our death. In some ways, we mime it in anticipation. After all, if we look at the face of elderly people with brain injuries, there is nothing scary or spectacular about them; there's no thundering, shimmering metamorphosis like in the myths. No, they are exactly the same as before, just with added indifference. That's what we look like, what we become in the memory of people who do not miss us, those who do not care. In everyone's memory, and no one's memory.

6

Is it possible to say "no"? A cut and dry "no" that is inconvertible to a "yes"? These questions make an ontology of the accident necessary. Is there a way for life to say no to itself? No to continuity; no to the resistance of memory or childhood; no to beautiful form; no to sensible metamorphosis; no to gradual decline; no to the progress of the negative itself? These questions can be summed up in a single question: is there a mode of possibility attached exclusively to negation? A possibility of a type that is irreducible to what appears to be the untransgressable law of possibility in general, namely affirmation. Is destructive plasticity possible?

Usually the notion of possibility is structurally linked to affirmation. To affirm is to say it is possible. Conversely, to say it is possible is always to affirm. Possibility designates what one is capable of, what may come into being, what may persist in being. By definition, possibility affirms itself as possible and this tautology comes back to the exclusion of the negative. In Kant's *Critique of*

Practical Reason, one of the finest texts ever written on possibility, we find luminous proof of this point on the topic of the originary nature of conscience in the moral law:

> ask him whether, if his prince demanded, on the threat of the same prompt penalty of death, that he give false testimony against an honest man whom the prince would like to ruin under specious pretenses, he might consider it possible to overcome his love of life, however great it may be. He will perhaps not venture to assure us whether or not he would overcome that love, but he must concede without hesitation that doing so would be possible for him.[88]

Of course, Hegel pointed out the contradictory form of this reasoning. Humans lay claim to the possibility of absolute negation. Can you say no? No to everything? No to life? Yes, I can do that. From then on, freedom becomes tied to the possibility of saying yes to no. Absolute negation is thus affirmative in principle. This claim then prompts Hegel to show that all possibility tends towards effectiveness, that all negation is confounded with the energy of its doubling, in other words, its positive power, its power of affirmation. Henceforth, if saying no always amounts to positing the possibility of something, it is no longer possible simply to negate. Categorical refusal is not possible.

Does negation have any chance at all then? The possibility I am trying to bring to light—how to say no, a cut and dry no, an inconvertible, irredeemable no; how to think destruction without remission—could be called the *negative possibility*. This type of possibility is not the negation of possibility, nor is it to be confused with the impossible. Without reducing it to affirmation, the negative possibility is not the expression of any lack or any deficit. It bears witness to a power or aptitude of the negative that is neither affirmed nor lacking, a power that *forms*. As I indicated, to take on the search for such a possibility immediately situates the proposal both within and without the yes and the no, even within and without the positive and the negative as traditionally understood.

Will we find the answer in the psychic attitude that consists in answering with neither a yes nor a no, in the very specific affective and intellectual gesture Freud terms "denegation" (*Verneinung*)?[89] Might denegation characterize the logical mode of action specific to destructive plasticity?

Is denegation the most appropriate term for referring to the negative possibility? In both French and German "dénier" (deny) means nothing more than "nier" (deny): "to declare to be untrue, to reject as false, to withhold, to refuse,"[90] it says in the dictionary. As for negation, it is commonly defined as "the opposite or absence of something, a negative thing, the act of negating."[91] But as we know, Freud confers a new meaning on this term. Negation is the act whereby a subject refuses to recognize as his own a desire, feeling or object that he has repressed. The *Language of Psychoanalysis* defines negation as follows: "Procedure whereby the subject, while formulating one of his wishes, thoughts or feelings which has been repressed hitherto, contrives, by disowning it, to continue to defend himself against it."[92]

Can destructive plasticity thus be viewed as a form of negation? Are people who are brain injured, excluded from society, traumatized, caught in this psychic mechanism by protecting themselves against what happens to them, by refusing to see it, by placing their suffering at a distance?

Using negation, the individual says no—but this no is a yes. Freud tells us that after recounting a dream the patient says to the analyst: "You ask who this person in the dream can be. It's *not* my mother."[93] The psychoanalyst immediately interprets this statement as an admission: "it's my mother," holding that the more vehement the patient's denials of his interpretation, the more they betray an admission or affirmation. "That's not my mother." "Obviously, therefore, it is her."

Freud says that this method, which is based on a logical scandal—transforming negation into affirmation—"is very convenient." And he continues, "'What,' we ask [the patient], 'would you consider the most unlikely imaginable thing in that situation? What do you think was furthest from your mind at that time?' If the patient falls into the trap and says what he thinks is most incredible, he almost always makes the right admission."[94] Interpretation thus consists in systematically taking the opposite view from what the patient says. If the patient says no, we understand it as yes. So isn't psychoanalysis therefore fully occupied in denying negation?

The question appears to be settled. We cannot escape the circle presented above if negating and denying, however different they may be, can always be retrieved by an affirmation, if denying also means, in a sense, the impossibility of denying. The negative possibility, the existential possibility opened by destructive plasticity, could not be reduced to the mechanism of psychic refusal if this actually leads to a form of affirmation.

We must acknowledge, however, that Freud's argument is far more complex. Denegation is not a simple negation that can be converted into its opposite. If it were as simple as that, the analytic cure would be swift and easy. Certainly, denegation is a thwarted affirmation, an upside-down affirmation, but it is also something else. It persists as negation despite its obvious dimension of admission. The subject who denies is seen right through by the analysis, yet continues to negate, does not recognize the evidence. The proof ceases to be an exhibit and we face a wall of resistance that does not give way before any test of truth or reality. Even if the analyst causes the denied object to resurface, in this instance, the mother— "it's your mother"—he does not manage to make it present to the subject; he makes it return negated, that is, as a pure possibility. "It's your mother," says the analyst, but as the patient will not accept it, the mother becomes not effective, but probable. "That's possible," the patient answers, "but you're the one saying it." Neither present, nor absent. Simply possible. It maintains its reservation forever.

Have we not therefore identified negative possibility? Wouldn't this match exactly that which, simply suggested by the other, is held in ontological reserve, without the status of being there? Doesn't destructive plasticity form lives and psyches touched by the accident, through a perpetual reserving or withdrawal of self-presence?

No, not at all. Indeed, Freud calls what holds itself on the threshold of being the repressed. The link between denegation and repression is indissoluble: "Thus the content of a repressed image or idea can make its way into consciousness, on condition that it is *negated.* Negation is a way of taking cognizance of what is repressed; indeed it is already a lifting of the repression, though not, of course, an acceptance of what is repressed."[95] Denegation is not "an admission of the repressed." However, as we have seen, it is also an admission of repression, which removes it, in a sense, since it delivers the excluded object (saying "it's not my mother" in some ways amounts precisely to saying "it's her"). But destructive plasticity does not work from repression. The accident—trauma, catastrophe, injury—is not repressed. It is not relegated, not occulted, not admitted. The affective coldness and indifference of victims are not strategies of escape and do not correspond to the depth of the strata of negativity that Freud reveals by distinguishing between intellectual and affective negativity.

Freud declares that it is possible to accept something intellectually but not affectively. "We can see how in this the intellectual function is separated from the affective process."[96] There are therefore two types of negativity. One, affective and unconscious, coincides with the repression process. The other, intellectual, makes negativity a function of judgment: something is or is not. The second type of negativity follows from the first. Later in the text *Die Verneinung*, Freud goes on to analyze the relation between these two negativities, showing that logical negativity, at work in syntax, thought, and judgment, originates in the affective, infantile negativity from which it subsequently frees itself by repressing it in turn. Freud thus retraces the stages in the transfer of power from one negativity to another.

What do we do when we express a negative judgment? At a purely symbolic level, we repeat an ancient infantile gesture: excluding, putting outside, rejecting. The psychic origin of negation is then forgotten. Freud brings it back to life here. He starts by reminding us that the logical function of judgment is dual: attribution (an attribution judgment states that an attribute or property belongs to an object) and existence (the judgment decides whether such and such a thing exists or not in reality). All negativity originates in the "pleasure-ego." The origin of attribution judgment can be found in the tendency of the ego to eat what it believes to be good and to spit out what it believes to be bad.

> The attribute to be decided about may originally have been good or bad, useful or harmful. Expressed in the language of the oldest—the oral—instinctual impulses, the judgment is: "I should like to eat this," or "I should like to spit it out"; and, put more generally: "I should like to take this into myself and to keep that out." That is to say: "It shall be inside me" or "it shall be outside me." As I have shown elsewhere, the original pleasure-

ego wants to introject into itself everything that is good
and to eject from itself everything that is bad.[97]

When we formulate a negative judgment in logic, in
other words, when we pronounce the non-attribution of
such and such a predicate to such and such a substance,
we symbolically and intellectually repeat a primitive
gesture of excluding or spitting out. Negation thus has
a clear affective origin: rejection. The only possibility of
being that such and such an object has when it is judged
harmful or bad by the ego is that of being expelled from
being. Not reduced to non-being, but well and truly
thrown out of being. Excluded from the register of
beings. In this sense the repressed or denied is ontological
spit. A rejection from presence.

This rejection is not nothing either; it does not characterize negative possibility. Negative possibility does not
proceed either from rejecting or spitting out. Since the
accident is in no way interiorized by the victim, it remains
foreign to the fate of the psyche and is not integrated
into the history of the individual. The individual does
not reject the trauma outside of him- or herself and has
no desire in relation to it, wants neither to eat nor to
vomit it.

In Freud, rejection is not nothing since it requires
exclusion. It must also be repeatable. Analyzing the

second form of judgment—the judgment regarding existence—Freud shows that it is based on the very ancient need to ensure the permanence of the interior/exterior distinction. "To introject" what is good is to interiorize. To reject what is bad is to put it outside. But this demands that inside and outside be stable, real. Yet it is precisely this that the instances of accident discussed here no longer have. The subject must be able to reclaim the good thing when he wishes and to reject the bad thing when he wishes.

The other sort of decision made by the function of judgment—as to the real existence of something of which there is a presentation (reality-testing)—is a concern of the definitive pleasure-ego. It is now no longer a question of whether what has been perceived . . . shall be taken into the ego or not, but of whether something which is in the ego as a presentation can be re-discovered in perception (reality) as well. It is, we see, once more a question of *external* and *internal*. What is unreal, merely a presentation and subjective, is only internal; what is real is also there *outside*. In this stage of development regard for the pleasure principle has been set aside. Experience has shown the subject that it is not only important whether a thing . . . possesses the "good" attribute and so deserves to be taken into his ego, but also whether it is there in the external world, so that he can get hold of it whenever he needs it.[98]

According to Freud, the ego needs to reassure itself regarding the reality of the outside. In order for the "pleasure-ego" truly to be able to throw out or reject something, the exclusion must necessarily appear to be definitive. What is rejected must not be able to return. What the subject is assured of is not the presence of that which is excluded, but rather the exclusion of what is excluded from presence. A phantasmatic, or even fantastic, reality of the remainder object. To say "that does not exist" would originally mean "the existence of this thing is excluded." Presence is only tolerated in so far as it is ontologically prohibited. Again, the reality of the mother in Freud's example is a non-presentable reality. "My mother is outside of presence"—a possibility without reality. Negation enables the subject to stand at the crossroads of two contradictory attitudes: to hide openly, or to dissimulate unknowingly.

In contrast to this double attitude, the negative possibility is that which the subject will not or cannot do, with inclusion and exclusion losing all meaning here. At the end of his text, Freud does appear to approach this type of situation of loss. If negation cannot be reduced to an inverse affirmation, if it truly gives negativity a chance, that is because it is impossible to know whether negation is active or passive, whether it is a deliberate occultation or not, and whether the patient can cease denying it. However much the psychoanalyst suggests the presence of the object, the patient in no way accepts the psychoanalytical hypothesis; he allows for it without accepting it. He holds onto his negation. And there's nothing to be done about it. Freud's late texts are absolutely clear about this. Negation can go so far as "forclusion" (*Verwerfung*), in other words, up to the refusal by the patient to become aware of their own resistance. Moreover, the 1925 text closes with the development of two groups of drives. Freud writes: "Affirmation—as a substitute for uniting—belongs to Eros; negation—the successor to expulsion—belongs to the instinct of destruction." And he continues by stating that this explains "the negativism which is displayed by some psychotics."[99] In these extreme cases, the negative possibility is purely and simply confused with the destruction drive. Negativity becomes annihilation.

But this danger of transforming negation into the impulse to destroy or annihilate does not cause Freud to capitulate and to admit the existence of destructive plasticity. Annihilation does not triumph. Rejection, non-presence retains its meaning. The excluded, the ontological pariahs, are not "nothing." It's their psychoanalytic chance. What does this chance, which so distances psychoanalysis from a neurological theory of trauma, depend on? What is it the chance for? What does it still allow to be preserved, that is, affirmed?

We must return to the structural link that connects possibility and denegation. The negative possibility—what must not come into presence—opens, alongside the affirmative possibility—which here is the affirmative possibility of the analyst ("but yes, of course, it is your mother, it is entirely possible that it is her, it is certain that it's her")—a cleavage that gives it its future. Denial always involves an act of faith, a faith that may be defined as faith in another possible beginning, a source other than the real historical source of what really happened. When I deny something, in other words, when I negate the evidence, I postulate, without being able to affirm it, that everything could have been otherwise, that everything could have happened differently. For example, I could have had another mother, another origin. "That's not her, my mother" would then mean "My mother, it's not her, the one that you think; there's another one. There could have been another one." Unwittingly, negation frees up the possibility of another story.

What is denied, the state of what must not be made present, reveals the existence of the secret question, the question that cannot be asked and which, at the same time, cannot but be asked for any psyche: what if something else had happened, anything else, something unexpected, something absolutely different from everything that happened? That's exactly what we cannot know. It's also what cannot not be taken as possible.

Isn't that which is rejected and excluded always, one way or another, the vertigo of the wholly other origin? Isn't what is spit out always what I am not and that which uncannily bears the question of what I could have been? The prohibited question that is negatively possible that shelters in the heart of any story, any translation, any genesis. Not what is going to be, but what could have been. This question that was scorned by Hegel in the name of effectiveness, and yet which exists in terms of negation. Denegation is born in this strange place where the concept of birth itself trembles. The question of the entirely other origin is a question that insists, digs, overflows the effective possible that is usually too readily dismissed: "don't think about what could have been," "look at the situation," "you can't remake history." And yet, don't we always think about the other possibility? Necessity's other? About this other origin that we hold to be negatively possible? What should we do with this threshold of non-presence that doubles the present, this negative halo that surrounds effectiveness with what could have been, since it keeps coming back?

On the one hand this return clearly signifies the implacable harshness of the negative, which Freud calls the repetition compulsion. In bringing back the scene of the trauma, we simultaneously bring back its denegation, that is, the possibility that nothing happened. Any question we throw out towards the wholly other, whether or not it be formulated and explicit—"And what if it hadn't happened? And what if something else had happened?"— would be a modality of the repetition compulsion, a blind, automatic procedure, the product of a resaying or redoing machine.

At the same time, on the other hand, the question of the other possibility, the wholly other version, is not simply witness to a compulsive, mechanical return; it also betrays an expectation, the expectation of the arrival of another way of being. A way of being excluded from reality. The way of being of the promise, of a to come that always lies in reserve. What is rejected, what is excluded, what is denied, is a possibility in waiting, a surprise resource.

With negation it is thus a question of the opening without a story in the story, of what Freud also called in *Inhibitions, Symptoms and Anxiety*, the "undoing."[100] In one sense, this not-happened, this non-place, this repressed or vomited, shelters within it the possibility of the worst. All nostalgia and all resentment are no doubt rooted in it. To try to actualize an assumed fantastic origin, to want to give rights to what could have been, to transform it into what must be, is a violent psychic gesture. To try to bring into being that which reality excluded from the start can coincide with the impulse to destroy, with the death drive.

But at the same time, this attitude is an attitude of minimizing evil. If negation cannot be touched by any revelation, any proof, any presence, if it always resists the trial of fact, it is in as much as it betrays an immense confidence. A naïve, absolute confidence, a child's faith in possibility, a fragile but unconditional belief without which existence would quite simply not be possible.

The possibility I seek to unearth is precisely the possibility that makes existence impossible. Isn't the possibility of denegation, this tenacious, unshakeable faith in the wholly other origin, the possibility of destructive plasticity, which refuses the promise, belief, symbolic constitution of all resources to come? It is not true that the structure of the promise is undeconstructible. The philosophy to come must explore the space of this collapse of messianic structures.

The Freudian discovery of denegation no doubt marks a decisive step in the analysis of this collapse, in the thought of destruction in general. However, as we have just seen, it still remains strongly attached to salvation, to redemption, to a type of psychic messianism, at the very moment when, paradoxically, it allows for the hypothesis of a negative therapeutic reaction. To refuse to allow for resistances is to believe that everything is still possible, it is to believe in the wholly other origin and to hang on to this idea. Destructive plasticity prohibits envisaging precisely the *other possibility*, even if it were an *a posteriori* possibility. It has nothing to do with the tenacious, incurable desire to transform what has taken place, to reengage in the history of the phantasm of an other history; it does not match any unconscious tactical strategy of opening, the refusal of what is, in the name of what could have been.

The denegation that accompanies anosognosia—a brain pathology whereby patients are unable to recognize themselves as ill—is not denegation in the Freudian sense. When the patient does not see that his left side is paralyzed, when he feels neither pain nor anxiety after a major brain injury, he is not responding to an affective imperative of unconsciously calculated blindness. He does not see because he cannot see, that's all.

Destructive plasticity deploys its work starting from the exhaustion of possibilities, when all virtuality has left long ago, when the child in the adult is erased, when cohesion is destroyed, family spirit vanished, friendship lost, links dissipated in the ever more intense cold of a barren life.

The negative possibility, which remains negative until it is exhausted, never becomes real, never becomes unreal either, but remains suspended in the post-traumatic form of a subject who misses nothing—who does not even lack lack, as Lacan might have written—remains to the end this subjective form that is constituted starting from the absence from the self. No psychoanalytic development of negativity is currently able to approach this possibility.

Go find in the great chest of metamorphosis something to dress and embody this ego that emerges from unthinkable nothingness, this enigma of a second birth that is not rebirth. Herein lies the philosophical difficulty that accompanies the thought of an eventness and a causal regime of unprecedented events, which owe nothing, paradoxically, to the thought of the event or to any theory of psychic etiology. By installing the relation of being and the accident outside any concept of psychic predestination, by marking the importance of the brutal and unexpected arrival of catastrophe, I do not seek to ward over a thought of the pure event or an idolatry of surprise. Quite the opposite: I refuse to believe that the accident responds to the call of an identity which, in a sense, is only waiting for it to unfurl. I know definitively, resolutely, that "it is dangerous to essenciate."[101] Not only because essentializing is a steamroller that levels accidents only imperfectly—so that accidents always threaten to damage essence itself *a posteriori*. But even more, and especially because, contrary to what Heidegger claims,[102] the history of being itself consists perhaps of nothing but a series of accidents which, in every era and without hope of return, dangerously disfigure the meaning of essence.

1 Marcel Detienne and Jean-Pierre Vernant, *Cunning Intelligence in Greek Culture and Society*, trans. Janet Lloyd, Hassocks, Sussex: Atlantic Highlands, NJ: Harvester Press, 1978, p. 20.

2 Cf. Jean-Pierre Vernant, *L'individu, la mort, l'amour: soi-même et l'autre en Grèce ancienne*, Paris: Gallimard, 1989, p. 29.

3 Detienne and Vernant, *Cunning Intelligence in Greek Culture and Society*, pp. 112–13.

4 Ibid., p. 113.

5 Sigmund Freud, "Instincts and their Vicissitudes" (1915), in *Standard Edition of the Complete Psychological Works of Sigmund Freud*, Vol. 14, trans. and ed. J. Strachey, in collaboration with A. Freud, assisted by A. Strachey and A. Tyson, London: Hogarth Press, 1954, p. 119.

6 Sigmund Freud, "Repression," in ibid, pp. 141–58, p. 155.

7 Ovid, *Metamorphoses I–IV*, Book 1, lines 549–52, trans. D. E. Hill, Illinois: Bolchazy-Carducci Publishers, Inc., 1985.

8 Antoni Casas Ros, *Le Théorème d'Almodovar*, Paris: Gallimard, 2008, p. 13 (my translation).

9 Ibid.

10 Catherine Malabou, *Les Nouveaux Blessés, de Freud à la neurologie: Penser les traumatismes contemporains*, Paris: Bayard, 2007;

The New Wounded: From Neurosis to Brain Damage, trans. Steven Miller, New York: Fordham, 2012.

11 Maurice Blanchot, *De Kafka à Kafka*, Paris: Gallimard, 1981, p. 73 (my translation).

12 Gilles Deleuze and Félix Guattari, *Kafka: Toward a Minor Literature*, trans. Dana Polan, Minneapolis: University of Minnesota Press, 1986, p. 14.

13 Ibid., p. 36.

14 Ibid., p. 14.

15 Ibid., p. 39.

16 Ibid., p. 6.

17 Cf. Gilles Deleuze and Félix Guattari, *A Thousand Plateaus: Capitalism and Schizophrenia*, trans. Brian Massumi, London: Continuum, 1987, pp. 291–310.

18 For more on Freudian "examples" of the death drive, see *The New Wounded*, Chapter 10.

19 Spinoza, *Ethics*, trans. G. H. R. Parkinson, Oxford: Oxford University Press, 2000, p. 169.

20 Antonio Damasio, *Looking for Spinoza: Joy, Sorrow, and the Feeling Brain*, Orlando, FL: Harcourt, 2003, p. 174.

21 Spinoza, *Ethics*, p. 165.

22 Ibid., p. 171.

23 Ibid., p. 209 (translation modified).

24 Antonio Damasio, *The Feeling of What Happens: Body and Emotion in the Making of Consciousness*, New York: Harcourt Brace, 1999, p. 41.

25 Ibid., pp. 41–2.

26 Ibid., p. 41. Doctor Xavier Emmanuelli, who founded the *SAMU social* (the French municipal emergency medical assistance service), also describes the characteristics common to all

trauma victims, even if their problems derive from different sources. See in particular *Out. L'exclusion peut-elle être vaincue?* Paris: Robert Laffont, 2003.

27 Damasio, *Looking for Spinoza*, p. 12.

28 Ibid., p. 36.

29 Ibid., pp. 36–7.

30 "Dupuy, le terrifiant récit," *La République des Pyrénées*, November 8, 2005 (my translation).

31 Damasio, *Looking for Spinoza*, pp. 140–1.

32 Spinoza, *Ethics*, pp. 255–6.

33 Ibid., pp. 256–7.

34 Ibid., p. 256.

35 Gilles Deleuze, *Expressionism in Philosophy: Spinoza*, trans. Martin Joughin, Cambridge, MA: MIT Press, 1990, p. 221.

36 Ibid., p. 222.

37 Ibid.

38 Ibid.

39 Ibid.

40 Cf. Joseph LeDoux, *Synaptic Self: How Our Brains Become Who We Are*, London: Penguin, 2002.

41 Spinoza, *Ethics*, p. 167.

42 Gérard Le Gouès, *L'Âge et le principe de plaisir. Introduction à la clinique tardive*, Paris: Dunod, 2000, p. 14 (my translation).

43 Ibid., p. 23 (my translation).

44 Sigmund Freud, "Thoughts for the Times on War and Death" (1915), in *Standard Edition of the Complete Psychological Works of Sigmund Freud*, Vol. 14, pp. 273–2, pp. 285–6.

45 Sigmund Freud, *Three Case Histories*, New York: Macmillan, 1963, p. 275.

46 Cited by Le Gouès, *L'Âge et le principe de plaisir*, p. 2 (my translation).

47 Ibid., p. 8 (my translation).

48 Freud, "Thoughts for the Times on War and Death," p. 286.

49 LeDoux, *Synaptic Self*, p. 307.

50 Le Gouès, *L'Âge et le principe de plaisir*, p. 10 (my translation).

51 Marcel Proust, *Finding Time Again*, in *In Search of Lost Time*, trans. Ian Patterson, London: Allen Lane, Penguin Press, 2002, p. 229.

52 Ibid., p. 234.

53 Ibid., pp. 245–6

54 Ibid., p. 243.

55 Ibid.

56 Ibid.

57 Ibid., p. 231.

58 Spinoza, *Ethics*, p. 256.

59 Proust, *Finding Time Again*, p. 231.

60 Ibid., p. 232.

61 Marguerite Duras, *The Lover*, trans. Barbara Bray, Glasgow: Collins Publishing Group, 1985, p. 7.

62 Ibid., pp. 7–8.

63 Marguerite Duras, *Practicalities: Marguerite Duras speaks to Jérôme Beaujour*, trans. Barbara Bray, New York: Grove Weidenfeld, 1990, p. 16.

64 Ibid., p. 12.

65 Duras, *The Lover*, p. 32.

66 Duras, *Practicalities*, pp. 16–17. On this point see Vincent Jaury's article, "Duras et 'la permanence de la blessure,'" *THS. La revue des addictions*, Vol. VII, No. 26, 2005, pp. 1338–40.

67 Duras, *Practicalities*, p. 16.

68 Ibid.

69 Ibid.

70 Marguerite Duras, *The Sailor from Gibraltar*, trans. Barbara Bray, London: Calder, 1966, pp. 254–5.

71 Georges Molinié and Michèle Acquien, *Dictionnaire de rhétorique et de poétique*, Paris: LGF, 1996, p. 350 (my translation).

72 Ibid.

73 Marguerite Duras, *Moderato Cantabile*, trans. Richard Seaver, in *Four Novels by Marguerite Duras*, New York: Grove Press, 1965, p. 99. The lack of liaisons became an almost caricatural feature of Duras' writing. In Patrick Rambaud's two parodies of Duras, signed Marguerite Duraille, *Virginie Q.* (Balland, 1998) and *Mururoa mon amour* (Jean-Claude Lattès, 1996), his satire constantly foregrounds asyndeton: "He does it. The black is dark in the room. It's a little like when you close your eyes. It's scary. She's scared." (*Virginie Q.*, p. 60, my translation.) Cf. Véronique Montemont, "Marguerite Duras vue par la statistique lexicale," ATILF, February 4, 2005, for examples of asyndeton.

74 Marguerite Duras, *The Sea Wall*, trans. Herma Briffault, New York: Farrar, Straus and Giroux, 1967, p. 197.

75 Duras, *The Lover*, p. 121.

76 Duras, *The Sea Wall*, p. 20.

77 Duras, *L'Amant*, Paris: Editions de Minuit, 1980, p. 31 (my translation).

78 Ibid., p. 58 (my translation).

79 Ibid., p. 49.

80 Duras, *Un Barrage contre le Pacifique*, Paris: Gallimard, 1978, p. 45 (my translation).

81 Duras, *The Lover*, p. 61.

82 Ibid., p. 17.

83 Ibid., p. 111.

84 Duras, *Practicalities*, p. 20.

85 Thomas Mann, *Buddenbrooks*, trans. H. T. Lowe-Porter, New York: Vintage, 1984, pp. 543–4.

86 Ibid., p. 551.

87 Pierre Marty, *Les Mouvements individuels de vie et de mort. Essai d'économie psychosomatique*, Payot, 1976, p. 71 (my translation).

88 Immanuel Kant, *Critique of Practical Reason*, trans. Werner S. Pluhar, Indianapolis: Hackett Publishing Company, Inc., 2002, p. 44.

89 Sigmund Freud, "Negation" (1925), in *Standard Edition of the Complete Psychological Works of Sigmund Freud*, Vol. 19, 1957, pp. 235–9.

90 *Dictionnaire Robert*.

91 Ibid.

92 Jean Laplanche and Jean-Baptiste Pontalis, *The Language of Psychoanalysis*, trans. Donald Nicholson-Smith, New York: Norton & Company, 1973, p. 261.

93 Freud, "Negation," p. 235.

94 Ibid.

95 Ibid., pp. 235–6.

96 Ibid., p. 236.

97 Ibid., pp. 236–7.

98 Ibid., p. 237.

99 Ibid., p. 239.

100 Sigmund Freud, "Inhibitions, Symptoms and Anxiety" (1926), in *Standard Edition of the Complete Psychological Works of Sigmund Freud*, Vol. 20, 1957, p. 119.

101 Henri Michaux, *Miserable Miracle*, trans. Louise Varese, New York: New York Review of Books, 2002, p. 143.

102 Cf., for example, Martin Heidegger, *Being and Time*, trans. John Macquarrie and Edward Robinson, Oxford: Blackwell, 1962, §81, p. 474: "It is no accident [*ist nicht zufällig*] that world time [authentic] thus gets leveled off and covered up by the way time is ordinarily understood [inauthentic]."